Engaging Empathy and Activating Agency

Engaging Empathy and Activating Agency

Young Adult Literature as a Catalyst for Action

Alice D. Hays

ROWMAN & LITTLEFIELD
Lanham • Boulder • New York • London

Published by Rowman & Littlefield
An imprint of The Rowman & Littlefield Publishing Group, Inc.
4501 Forbes Boulevard, Suite 200, Lanham, Maryland 20706
www.rowman.com

6 Tinworth Street, London SE11 5AL, United Kingdom

Copyright © 2021 by Alice D. Hays

All rights reserved. No part of this book may be reproduced in any form or by any electronic or mechanical means, including information storage and retrieval systems, without written permission from the publisher, except by a reviewer who may quote passages in a review.

British Library Cataloguing in Publication Information Available

Library of Congress Cataloging-in-Publication Data

Library of Congress Control Number: 2021932754

ISBN: 978-1-4758-5364-3 (cloth)
ISBN: 978-1-4758-5365-0 (pbk.)
ISBN: 978-1-4758-5366-7 (electronic)

*This book is dedicated to my mother, Shan,
and two daughters, Lorisa and Ellie.
Without their editing prowess, emotional support, constant encouragement,
and ability to bake their own cookies, this book would not have existed.*

Contents

Foreword *Dr. James Blasingame*	xi
Prologue	xv
Introduction	xvii
Why Young Adult Literature?	xvii
How Can Reading YAL Develop Empathy?	xviii
Why Is It Important to Teach for Agency?	xix
Who Did This Work?	xx
Acknowledgments	xxiii
1 Finding the Passion	1
What the Teacher Does	2
Priming Students for Issue Focus	2
Guiding Students through Privilege Activities	3
Identity	5
Finding Books	6
Thinking through It	7
Student Activities	9
Discussions of Privilege	9
Philosophical Chairs	9
Brainstorming Issues	10
Social Identity Wheel	10
Putting Theory into Practice	12
Successes	13
Struggles	14
Conclusion	14

2	Reading the Novels	17
	What the Teacher Does	18
	Creating Groups	18
	Setting up a Reading Timeline	19
	Thinking through It	19
	Consider Reading Attitudes	19
	Prepare Literature Circle Packets	20
	Student Activities	20
	Literature Circles	20
	Collaborative Note Taking	22
	Structured Identity Journal Entries	22
	Putting Theory into Practice	24
	Successes	25
	Struggles	28
	Conclusion	30
3	Building Capacity and Engaging Community	31
	What the Teacher Does	32
	Focusing the Research Question	32
	Understanding and Identifying Research Sources	33
	Making Connections	34
	Sharing Information	35
	Student Activities	35
	Preresearch Activities	35
	Secondary Research Activities	38
	Primary Research Activities	41
	Presentation Activities	44
	Putting Theory into Practice	45
	Successes	45
	Struggles	46
	Conclusion	47
4	Taking Action	49
	What the Teacher Does	50
	Student Agency	50
	Idea Bank	51
	School-Communication	52
	Conferencing with Student Groups	52
	Thinking through It	53
	Barriers Students Might Have around the Issues Themselves	53
	Troubleshooting and Supplying Innovative Approaches	54
	Student Activities	55
	Develop the Work Plan	55

	Present Results to Stakeholders in the Community	56
	Reach Out to School Administrators	58
	Present to the School	58
	Assessments	59
	Putting Theory into Practice	61
	Successes	61
	Struggles	61
	Conclusion	63
5	Voices from the Field	65
	Teacher 1: Mr. Muñoz	65
	Teacher 2: Ms. Neff	71
	Student Experience: Isaiah	76
Appendix: Books for Social Justice Issues		81
	Middle School Book Ideas	81
	Racism	81
	Poverty	81
	Immigration	82
	Drug Abuse	83
	Women's Rights	83
	Social Media Awareness	84
	Domestic Abuse/Violence	85
	Mental Health/Suicide	86
	Environment	86
	Bullying/Peer Pressure	87
	Human Trafficking	87
	High School Book Ideas	88
	Refugee/Immigration	88
	Muslim Discrimination	89
	Racial Equality	89
	Gender Equality	90
	LGBTQ	90
	Poverty	91
	Abuse	91
	Mental Health	92
	Environment	92
	Technology	93
	Bullying	94
Works Cited		95
About the Author		101

Foreword

Dr. James Blasingame

Dr. Alice Hays has always been a passionate teacher—passionate about her subject matter, passionate about her teaching methods, and most importantly, passionate about her students. As a high school English teacher, she was much beloved by students and parents for her attention to every student's needs, and much respected by her colleagues and school administrators for her devotion to staying up-to-date on teaching and learning research and practice. She was adept at inciting passion among her students for learning, which resulted in literacy proficiencies that helped to put her school at the top of performance measures in the state. Every year at the Arizona English Teachers Association Convention, teachers would flock to her presentations on how she was implementing new literacies, global education, young adult literature, and new technologies.

Perhaps greatest of all her passions revolved around students learning literacy skills designed to serve them well in real life—skills that would empower them to choose their own path in life and to make the world a better place. This book is all about that very thing: empowering students to make the world and their own lives better through curriculum and instruction that will help them in their life journeys, whether that be medicine or law, engineering or construction, civil service or military, or social work or education, whatever path they choose to take. Developing imagination about a world and life that could be, personal agency, and commitment to purpose are at the center of identified student goals in this book.

Real-world literacy requires reading, writing, and research curriculum for the 2020s. Research always begins with questions, sometimes hard questions, and secondary students already have so many. Why do so many of our peers commit suicide, and what can we do about it? Why do so many young soldiers face such difficulty in returning to civilian life, and how can we help? Why is bullying so prevalent in our society, and what can we do about it? Why does our state rank forty-sixth in the nation for childhood well-being? Young people can feel powerless in a world they see as damaged, but feelings of helplessness morph into feelings of empowerment and, in the end, productive action using Dr. Hays's curriculum. "Encourage them to follow their hearts," she says (page 33), provide them with the tools they need, and guides them in the areas they need help.

The old school research paper unit has students looking up preapproved topics in the school or public library electronic card catalog, following the usual steps to create notecards, thesis statements, pro and con arguments, and conclusions, and finally writing the usual, predictable, formulaic final paper. Quite the opposite, Dr. Hays begins with the most powerful activity that can be done in class—fiction reading. A book is a powerful thing, and studies clearly show that reading self-selected fiction is not only one of the fastest ways to improve reading skills, but it also has a measurable effect on the ability to empathize with other human beings, especially those who come from a life very different from the readers (Skinner 2016). As former director of the Beverly Hills Library and past president of the Young Adult Library Services Association says, "You can give a young reader statistics on alcoholism in dysfunctional families, but if you want them to understand how it feels to be in that family, give them the young adult (YA) novel *Make Lemonade*, by Virginia Euwer Wolf. Empathy makes us human and inspires us to help our fellow human beings."

As Hays points out, real reading means more than just following a story, more than just emotionless dissection of characters and charting of conflict and theme. Well-written YA fiction invites readers into the story as participants, and the action unit plan invites them to examine themselves, their beliefs, their biases, their strengths, and their vulnerabilities. It also moves them to examine the world around them, from local to global, from the powerful to the powerless—all from the safe distance of literature. These are books that affect students' hearts as well as their intellect. And YA fiction includes books that resonate with any and every possible reader, centering on every problem there could happen in a young person's life (see WeNeedDiverseBooks at https://diversebooks.org/). Approximately 4,000 new YA books come out every year from publishing houses of all kinds, from HarperCollins to Cinco Puentos, from Scholastic to Arte Público.

Every successful teacher knows that scaffolding teaching activities thoughtfully is key to good delivery of instruction, and Dr. Hays provides multiple choices for teachers and students to move the class from point A (generating a list of topics of concern) to point Z (implementing the action plan). For example, she provides a variety of ways that students can read and discuss (e.g., lists and explanations of various reading strategies, how to use literature circles, when to use audiobooks, and how to implement collaborative note-taking), a variety of ways students can interact (how to choreograph philosophical chairs, how to use a social identity wheel, and how to teach students effective annotation), and a variety of ways they can respond to their reading in order to rise to what Applebee et al. (2003) called "high literacy acts" (problem trees, interviews, finding allies). In addition, choice is highly valued here; student choices are so important: choice of issue/topic, choice of YA fiction book, choice of learning activities, and choice of action plan format. And the results make learning a new curriculum design and instructional delivery system worth it.

Every chapter provides a roadmap created by Dr. Hays, who has not only created and taught this unit herself but has also done qualitative data analysis on the successes and challenges of others who have tried it. In each chapter, teachers will find a section on what they do in each step of the unit in the form of multiple options. This is followed by a little troubleshooting from a veteran who can predict where things might get off-track and how to avoid pitfalls or solve problems. In each chapter, there are assorted resources listed (NewsELA, NPR.org, and more), followed by choice after choice of what the students can do at this point in the project from which the teacher may choose—including choices to provide to the students themselves. Each chapter ends with "Putting Theory into Practice," a sort of user-friendly manual for those in the trenches. The book ends with an appendix providing lists of books by topic and reading level so that teachers who are not already reading several YA books a month can benefit from Dr. Hays's expertise.

As the book ends, Dr. Hays shares the thoughts and feelings of teachers and students, in their own words, about what the impact of the unit was in their lives. What did she learn from the teachers? That students buy into their education when the teacher shares the reins. Teachers also say that the skill-building takes on a new dimension when it is the road to a destination students are passionate to reach. Teachers are still glowing about the personal changes they saw in students in their confidence and self-worth, in their performance, in their ability to make their way in the world. They see their students successfully taking on responsibility for their own lives and their community's well-being. The students, themselves, graduate knowing that the right book can change lives, even save them, and that reading can be a meaningful and enjoyable activity. They learn that following their hearts with the help of their minds really can change their lives for the better, and even make the world a better place for everyone.

REFERENCE

Skinner, J. (April 21, 2016). "Miranda McKearney and the Power of Reading: Pleasure, Empathy and Social Justice." National Library of New Zealand.

Prologue

"So, what do we have to do in order to earn an A in this class?"

This question, asked quite benignly, was the opening day to my first semester as a dual credit English teacher. Students in this class were going to earn college credit and high school credit and were some of the brightest students on the campus. Of course, they wanted A's—these were the students who were college-bound and willing (and able) to pay money for a high school course so they could get ahead in life. What I hadn't expected was a singular focus only on the percentage points and a complete lack of interest in the learning prospects of the class.

This felt a bit like a dagger in my heart, because who doesn't love English class, just because it's amazing? As I tried to talk them into the exciting prospects of a composition class, I realized that I, myself, wasn't a hundred percent sure of the ultimate purpose of writing these various, disconnected essays. It was at that point that I realized I had to come up with a different approach.

I landed on a solution—activism! I centered my entire school year around the idea that each of their assignments would propel them toward the creation of an action plan of their own choosing. They selected an issue they wanted to deal with, and after grappling with the issue through reading, writing, and speaking skills, they ultimately generated a solution that they could enact locally. This transformed my class. No longer were students simply writing to get an A. They were writing to change the world. And no longer was the classroom centered around me but instead my students and their passions. I felt as if I had reached the pinnacle of teaching success.

As I began my study of young adult literature (YAL), I wondered how I could couple this civic engagement that worked so well with my composition students with my newfound passion for YAL. In watching my own daughter read *Out of My Mind*, by Sharon Draper (2012), I saw her become so emotionally frustrated with the storyline in the book that she ripped a page out of the novel and threw the book across the room! This is absolutely not how we treat books at our house. But this did inspire me to focus on how we might channel that energy into more positive behavior, which led me to work with some amazing teachers, and ultimately to the development of this book.

Thanks to the incredibly open and thoughtful work of educators in Arizona and in California, we co-created this curriculum that focuses on student-selected issues, YAL, and ultimately pro-social behavior. Each teacher that has developed this curriculum has continued to implement it into their classes multiple times, and they each are eager to explain how much they enjoy the added level of engagement in their courses. I am excited to share this work with you.

Through the effective pairing of YAL with a pro-social behavior, I believe we can transform educational spaces and the learning of students. May this curriculum support those endeavors.

Introduction

Teaching for social responsibility with good books does far more than encourage civic participation; it redefines the purpose of school and empowers all of us—students, teachers, administrators, parents—to be better people and live more fulfilling lives.

—Steven Wolk (2009, 664)

WHY YOUNG ADULT LITERATURE?

YAL has been recognized for its ability to explore and discuss complex topics in ways that are accessible to adolescents and allow them to thoughtfully reflect, develop empathy, and learn about important social issues (Buckley-Marudas and Ellenbogen 2019; Pytash et al. 2014; Connors 2017). YAL has had a relatively recent emergence and as such is still in the fledgling stages of being defined. While Nilsen et al. (2013) defined YAL as books that were being chosen by adolescents, the preponderance of books written for this age group has grown, along with the popularity of the novels across all ages, which demands that more stringent parameters be placed upon this type of literature. As such, I propose to utilize Malo-Juvera and Hill's (2020) definition of YA for the purposes of this book. They determine that the narratives of YA "enable close identification, engendering empathy, particularly with the narrator and/or protagonist" (n.p.). Additionally, they pull on Trites's (2000) and Coats's (2011) explication that YAL takes on a critical stance of societal norms. It is through this self-identification that students are able to put themselves into situations they may or may not experience in their day to day lives.

As students self-identify with aspects of characters, they are better able to put themselves into the shoes of people who have vastly different experiences than themselves. One such example was demonstrated with a young woman who had always had a somewhat critical view of poverty in that she believed it was entirely avoidable. However, the student identified with the social awkwardness experienced by Eleanor from *Eleanor & Park* (Rowell 2015), and subsequently changed her perception of people in poverty in significant ways. Seeing a character for whom she felt an affinity experiencing poverty through no fault of her own caused her to rethink her assignment of blame, at least momentarily.

Since identity is often shaped by social and cultural forces (Beach et al. 2015; Thein et al. 2012; Gee 2001), the books students read can have a significant impact on the way they view themselves. Students who see themselves mirrored in the book may experience a sense of self-affirmation (Bishop 1990). And students who see "others" in books may also develop a higher level of understanding, leading to a more connected society, ideally.

Another reason YAL is important to this curriculum is that students will need to have books they can and want to read independently, since focused choice is a critical component of this curriculum. As the teacher, you will not be able to guide your students through their various books as a whole class, so they must become more independent readers.

YAL does have this power to get students to identify as readers (Gay, Ivey and Johnston 2013; Gay, Ivey and Broaddus 2001), without bringing out the cattle prods and whips. While it may seem difficult to release control of this portion of the class, students who are allowed to find their own meaning in literacy work are often more successful (Applebee et al. 2003), and students who begin a choice project with a driving question or purpose are also more likely to be successful (Goodwin 2010). In my research, I have experienced the joy of students seeing me in their classroom and excitedly asking the teacher if they get to do YAL right now. The students I have observed seem to truly see doing this work as more of an adventure than a chore, which brings joy to my heart.

HOW CAN READING YAL DEVELOP EMPATHY?

We are living in a time when empathy is in short supply on the national stage. However, "the literary experience, intimately connected to the building of empathy, may be an essential part of slowing the spread of such social problems as bullying, school violence, and rampant uncivil discourse" (Alsup 2015, 6). If we are truly to shuttle in a kinder, gentler version of society in our future, it is critical that students have an understanding of humanity. Assisting students in developing empathy is one way to support our students.

Frans B. M. de Waal (2014) writes about chimpanzees and their ability to take emotional cues from one another from their body language and behaviors. He also states that the "more similar and socially close two individuals are," the easier it is to show empathy (de Waal 2014, 198). Alsup (2015) makes the argument that if we are to extract and apply this to adolescents, their ability to connect with stories might be better done with characters who look more like them, in age as well as in potential experience.

One way that teachers can support this development of empathy is through exposure to diverse YAL. In school, emotional rules come from classroom norms about what is appropriate. They may be informed by society's discourse and culture, but they are constructed and negotiated in specific social contexts (Thein et al. 2015). This was apparent when a young man who was shy and withdrawn in class read a novel where bullying was the focus, and ultimately created a non-bullying pledge for people, and approached strangers, to him, throughout the school and asked them to commit to the social contract. The classroom experience reframed the social construction around the normalcy of bullying.

Another young woman struggled to understand why anyone might do drugs, but after reading a novel about various types of abuse, she developed an understanding of the hopelessness behind the choices people might make. If teachers provide students with opportunities to read about people of their age who are going through similar or dissimilar issues, the social context can inspire students to develop empathy for others. The ability to understand one another is critical to our success as a society.

While empathy is important for our students to learn, it is not necessarily enough. While empathy has the potential to lead to pro-social or altruistic action (Keen 2006), adolescents often need scaffolded support to harness those emotions (Hays 2018).

WHY IS IT IMPORTANT TO TEACH FOR AGENCY?

Many of our students are experiencing issues in their personal lives that some of us cannot imagine. Using books that also talk about those same issues provides a way for students to see themselves, which, as Chris Crutcher often speaks about, can be a form of therapy. For those students who don't have those personal issues, these books can be valuable tools in helping them learn how to navigate their relationships with others who have different experiences. These books, ultimately, help kids deal with real life (Lesesne 2007).

In thinking about truly learning and understanding a new concept, most people would agree that merely reading and discussing an issue isn't enough. There are different types of talk that teachers use in a classroom, and it is critical that we move beyond simple regurgitation (Keene 2007; R. Probst 2007). One way to do this is by taking action toward solving an issue.

As Chin writes, "Children can and do produce knowledge that is worth paying attention to" (2007, 272). In the age of standardized testing, students do not often have the opportunity to show that they are knowledge-makers. Yet our primary goal as educators is to prepare students for their future. We are doing students a disservice if we are not providing them with opportunities to navigate the power structures in the world around them in ways that are safe and scaffolded.

There is an inherent culture of power (Delpit 2006) that exists in schools and in society, and providing students with opportunities for agency allows them to begin to understand how to shift the political landscape (Cammarota 2011). Participating in society will not be a series of tests that students take to prove their knowledge, but instead the ability to identify issues within their communities that need to be addressed and figuring out how to enact change. "Positioning youth as doers and knowledge generators within the space of the classroom promotes shared responsibility and empathy, which are precursors to affiliation, belonging, and activist impulses" (Dejaynes and Curmi 2015, 78).

We live in a society that is huge, and often-times feels disconnected. In order to feel a connection, it is important that we have a sense of empathy, but empathy without a drive to action can become debilitating. Students who understand how to make positive changes in their world will be more driven to participate actively within their society. And if we can make that happen within our classrooms, we will experience joyful, engaging experiences, where all the skills are being addressed while simultaneously addressing the social and emotional aspects of the whole child.

WHO DID THIS WORK?

The teachers who joined me in this work co-constructed this curriculum with me over time, and I am incredibly grateful to each of them. The first educator is Ms. Julie Neff who graciously opened up her tenth grade honors curriculum to do this work. She teaches in a suburban school that is fairly diverse, and she has a cross-section of students in her classroom. She has now followed this curriculum for four years and credits it with changing her approach to teaching. Over the years, she has added several ideas that show up in this text.

The second group of teachers was the seventh grade English Language Arts team, Mr. Muñoz, Mr. Flores, and Mr. Frost, at a rural school in the central valley of California. We met to plan the curriculum several times before they started the work, and their input about what they wanted to focus on for their students was invaluable. Helping these seventh graders truly find their voice while achieving academic success was at the core of each of their teaching philosophies, although each teacher adapted slightly different approaches to the work. Their experiences are discussed in each chapter, and I hope that they provide ideas for you to modify the curriculum in necessary and important ways.

Through the effective pairing of YAL with a pro-social behavior, I truly believe we can transform educational spaces and the learning of students. May this curriculum and these teachers' stories support those endeavors.

Acknowledgments

There are so many people who participated in the creation and development of this book, without whom this book would not have existed. Most critically, the educators who thought my idea sounded interesting and were willing to let me come into their classes and provided feedback for this curriculum.

Thank you, Anthony Celaya, for being willing to be the first guinea pig and giving me access to such brilliant and amazing students who helped me see the potential for what we could do with this.

Thank you to Julie Neff, who not only opened up her classroom doors and her class calendar to my ideas but also inspired me with her own spin and approach to this work. Because of your wise tweaks and additions, this curriculum is ready to share. I appreciate your enthusiasm for every conference proposal I ask you about, and your constant desire to be the absolute best teacher you can be for your students!

Thank you to Christian Muñoz and the rest of the Lincoln Junior High seventh grade ELA team! You helped me see how multiple educators might take up this work, and your eagerness to advocate for your students is an inspiration.

And to those individuals who encouraged me and pushed me to "just lean forward and keep my feet moving," like Dr. James Blasingame, I owe you the sincerest debt of gratitude! Thank you for supporting my journey as a scholar! Thank you to my work family at California State University, Bakersfield (CSUB) for being unwaveringly supportive and inspirational and to my many writing group partners, most especially Dr. Maria Hernandez-Goff, Dr. Bre Evans-Santiago, and Shan Hays, my earliest editor. And thank you to Dan Shanyfelt for giving me the push to get started. I needed that. Vickie Spanos was always an incredible cheerleader, and never once wavered in her enthusiasm around this work. I so appreciate you making me feel at home in the

Bakersfield community! Thank you to all of my family who inspires me to want to make the world a better place. A special thanks to Ellie and Lorisa for being such amazing children that I was able to do this work, almost guilt free!

Finally, thank you to my own Gilbert High School students. They willingly dove into the earliest renditions of this work and showed me the value and importance of giving students voice. It is through you that I truly learned how incredible, intelligent, and worldly young adults can be when given the choice to use their education experience to make the world a better place. You give me hope for a brighter future! And teachers who provide these opportunities for these students—thank you! You are making the world a little bit better through your guidance.

Chapter 1

Finding the Passion

Mrs. Hays, why do we even have to do this anyway? When are we ever going to use this in real life?

—Random student (any year)

Sadly, the response that knowing what the green light symbolizes in *The Great Gatsby* (Fitzgerald 1925) would be useful in trivia games didn't generate the passion one would hope for. This curriculum comes out of the critical need to have a stronger answer to this exact question.

While there is significant value in learning to think critically and being able to express one self through speaking and writing in ways that we teach in secondary literacy classes, students don't always see the immediate transferability of their learning. As a result, many students spend far too many years being complacent learners in their classroom without realizing why they are learning the material being covered. Additionally, students are rarely given the opportunity to drive their own education, even though they are fully capable of thinking critically about their educational experience (Raby 2007; Petrone and Sarigianides 2017).

While it may seem as though every school year provides you with a blank slate of new students to fill with knowledge, those students in front of you are not actually empty vessels. They often have a vast array of experiences that color their own education experience. Their consumption of social media often means they are far more exposed to an array of both local and global issues. As demonstrated by recent Nobel Peace Prize recipient and nominee, Malala Yousafzai and Greta Thunberg, respectively, adolescents are more than capable of thinking about and acting upon broad issues that exist outside their personal selves.

Table 1.1   Activity Overview

Teacher Does	Students Do
Introduce social justice through various articles and activities	Consider their varying degrees of privilege through various activities
Lead brainstorming activity	Generate list of issues they care about and begin to narrow their focus to one focal point
Lead students through discussion about Chimamanda Adichie's TED Talk, "Danger of a Single Story"	Work through Social Identity Wheel
Identify books that are appropriate based on issues students chose	Make a final decision about their issue, and potentially acquire the relevant novel

Note: Adichie's TED Talk can be found through a web search.

If education is intended to be a conduit for students to become productive members of society, it is imperative that teachers focus on the civic purpose of education, and allow students inroads to develop their abilities to participate in society in meaningful ways.

In order to begin this work, students need to consider and discuss their own positionality, identity, and their society around them so that they might thoughtfully consider how they can and would want to positively impact the world. This chapter will detail the steps that teachers must take in order to prepare students to begin the curriculum of reading for action by discussing how to read novels in a way that will generate both empathy and agency. Refer to table 1.1 for an overview of the activities.

WHAT THE TEACHER DOES

Priming Students for Issue Focus

Before asking students to take action on a social justice issue of their choice, it is important to prime them to either explore a world that is wider than they might have experienced prior to entering your classroom, or help them to draw upon their own experiences.

Nonfiction Articles

Since students are focusing on contemporary issues, connecting the class to current society through news articles will help to create the transfer and applicability of the class to "real life."

Social justice is often understood as an issue of "fairness" and "equality" for everyone (Sensoy and DiAngelo 2017). It will be useful to begin by presenting ideas about inequality in general terms. The *New York Times* published an interview between Gary Gutting and Elizabeth Anderson (2015), which discusses the various ways that one might define equality in general. This may be an important discussion to have with students as they begin to analyze and consider various issues that they may or may not be familiar with. This particular interview emphasizes the wide range and types of inequality that all sorts of individuals might experience.

Students who are unsure what topic they might be interested in focusing on may find that this article provides a solid foundation that may inspire further research. In addition to a general overview article, identifying two to three articles that deal with a variety of social justice issues will help students bridge the gap between fiction and reality. This may be particularly helpful to ground students in the importance of their issue as they move into reading their novel. These nonfiction articles have the added benefit of meeting the expectations of nonfiction in the ELA Common Core State Standards.

Guiding Students through Privilege Activities

Some students may benefit from exploring the guided privilege activities explicated later in the chapter. While there has been a video that recently went "viral" with a depiction of a privilege walk, I would caution you against implementing that approach with your students. This may cause some individuals to have to expose parts of their life that they may not be comfortable sharing with their peers in ways that may create problems in the classroom relationships.

Leading Brainstorming Activity—Once you have primed students to think about their own positionality, it is time to begin narrowing their focus on what they might want to change.

There are a number of issues that students might have experienced and or discussed throughout their lives prior to entering your classroom. The first activity you would want your students to do might be to brainstorm the types of issues that they see as problematic within their community. You might have them do this work individually, as a mini-research project, or as a class activity.

It is important that every student have a chance to identify the issues within their society that they are concerned with and would like to address. It is equally important to make sure that they understand that a social issue is one that is created or exacerbated by society, whether it is simply a reflection of social norms or specific policies that create the issues. While they may choose an issue that impacts them personally, they need to think about the issues' solutions in external terms.

Following are steps to help students narrow down the issues they choose in order to begin focusing their topics.

(1) Ask students to identify three to five issues they see as important individually. Give them five to ten minutes to do this work.
(2) Ask students to bring their sticky notes up to the board/wall/front of the room and begin clustering their issues together. Alternatively, if you do not want to use sticky notes, you might ask three to five students to write their issues on a whiteboard or chalkboard, then ask others to either make a tick mark by the issues they also identified, or create a new category on the board.
(3) Identify any outlying issues that don't seem to be clumped together. This would be an opportune time to allow students to pitch their issue to the rest of the class as being important enough to focus on. You can call for another show of hands of anyone who would like to join that issue, and add a tick mark to that topic, or eliminate it if no one else is willing to jump on board with that student. At this point, your goal will be to narrow the issues down to the top eight to ten topics, if possible. Through the next survey, the issues will be identified more specifically, so don't worry if you have many issues.
(4) Create a list of those topics for each different class with a blank line next to each topic. Make enough copies for everyone to have one paper. Refer to the textbox 1.1 for an example of what this might look like.
(5) Ask students to number their top three issues from 1 to 3, with 1 being the topic they are most passionate about, or most interested in solving/learning about. It is important that they do this, as if there are not enough people in the class to do the topic with them, you will have to give them a second or third topic choice.
(6) You will sort through the topics, and group the students together by topic. The groups should be of three to five students per topic. If ten students have all identified racism as their number 1 topic, you do not need to give some of them their second choice. You will simply have two groups who are focused on the idea of racism. If you have only two students who chose a topic, you will need to give them their second choice topic. Typically, students are able to get their first or second choice topic, which provides the students with a sense of ownership over what they are learning, and allows their voice to come through in their work.

TEXTBOX 1.1 TOPIC AND BOOK OF INTEREST SURVEY

Name: _____
Period: _____

Please rank the following topics from 1 to 10 according to your interest level in the topic and/or the book you will be reading, 1 being your first choice and 10 being your last choice. Then circle the books you have previously read.

_____ Racial equality—*All American Boys* by Jason Reynolds
_____ Gender equality—*The Boston Girl* by Anita Diamante
_____ Immigration—*The Circuit* by Francisco Jimenez
_____ LGBTQ—*Openly Straight* by Bill Koninsberg
_____ Poverty—*Eleanor & Park* by Rainbow Rowell
_____ Abuse—*Chinese Handcuffs* by Chris Crutcher
_____ Mental health—*It's Kind of a Funny Story* by Ned Vizzini
_____ Muslim discrimination—*Does My Head Look Big in This?* by Randa Abdel-Fattah
_____ Refugees—*The Good Braider* by Tery Farish
_____ Environmental—*Kingsley* by Carolyn O'Neal

If there is another issue you are interested in that is not on this list, please indicate below:

_____

Identity

Merriam-Webster defines identity as A: the distinguishing character or personality of an individual: individuality. B: the relation established by psychological identification ("Identity" 2020). In pedagogical terms, there are moves that you make as a teacher that support different identities your students take up. Gee (2001) writes that identity can be created and connected to affinity groups. These affinity groups can be created in the classroom. The ways that students develop identity is fluid, and a strong enough identification with a particular group may support more in-depth connections for students.

The ways that readers interact with literacies influences the identities that they take up (Moje et al. 2007) and the use of YAL with adolescents as protagonists can support students' ability to connect with the novel's characters and issues in ways that other readings may not. This sense of identification can broaden students' understanding of the world and subsequently the issue they chose.

Single Story—One way to prepare students to consider different identities or perspectives is by discussing the concept of a single story.

Chimamanda Adichie gave a Technology, Entertainment and Design (TED) Talk in July of 2009 titled "The Danger of a Single Story." In this TED Talk, she explores the experience she had as a college student from Nigeria. Adichie's favorite musical artist at the time was Mariah Carey, and her roommate was surprised that Adichie did not only listen to tribal music. Adichie was surprised to learn that her roommate had a single story about her, and realized that she had held her own single story about people from her childhood. This talk examines how dangerous it can be to see people through a single, often uninformed lens.

Following this video, it would be good to discuss the stereotypes or stories students have heard or experienced about people their age. This can also be used as a segue to begin discussion about the stories or perceptions they have about the topic or issue they chose to focus on. This will be helpful as they continue to read and learn about the characters, as well as while they conduct their research.

Another activity that may help them consider the ways that they think about themselves, as compared to the way that others think about them, might be facilitated through the social identity wheel activity discussed later in the chapter.

Finding Books

Finding books has been one of the most fun, yet also most difficult, steps in implementing this curriculum. Several wonderful websites offer thorough, useful reviews of books, and the appendix at the back of this book lists texts that have been used with some success. Table 1.2 offers several possible websites where you can search for book titles.

It is important to consider the reading levels, maturity levels, and accessibility issues for each of the novels. The most critical factor is that the novels themselves are YAL, in that they focus on an adolescent protagonist who is dealing with the issue in some way shape or form. Having characters who are of similar ages to the reader allows the reader to identify with the story in more in-depth ways. This identification can inspire a more thoughtful reflection about what they might do if they were in the situation, more acceptance of the issue if they have no prior experience, or even a sense of comfort in seeing their own issues mirrored in the novel.

Table 1.2 Websites to Find Books

www.yawednesday.org	Run by Dr. Steve Bickmore from University of Nevada, Las Vegas, this blog post details reviews of books, book lists for certain topics, and big ideas that are being discussed in the young adult literature world.
www.goodreads.com	This site is easily searchable, and provides many reviews that explain the topics of texts while giving an evaluative rating.
www.diversebooks.org /resources/	This website provides a searchable database that will pair your reader with books of their interest and reading level, all while focused on diverse authors and characters. (This fills in the publishing gap, as many books still feature predominantly white authors and characters, even as our student body diversity grows.)
www.yalsa.ala.org	The Young Adult Library Service Association publishes a yearly list of books that have been selected for young adults with detailed summaries.

Thinking through It

There are several issues that may arise at this point in the process. Some of them are organizational issues, and some may deal with the students themselves.

Resistance from students—Some students may be unwilling to think about social justice issues for a variety of reasons. It may be that it hits too close to home, or that they don't feel it is their responsibility to address issue that they may not see as affecting them. It is critical that students are given options in this case. If they have the freedom to choose an issue that impacts them, they will be more inclined to want to do the work necessary.

Sometimes students feel overwhelmed at the idea of having to identify a solution to the issue they have chosen and balk at the idea of picking a difficult topic. If this is the case, they should be reassured that their task will not be to solve the issue in its entirety, but simply to take steps to alleviate some aspect of the issue in different ways.

Resistance from teachers/administration—While you and your students may be ready to change the world, you may get push-back from teachers or administrators who feel that your students aren't emotionally prepared to tackle the issues that are difficult or hard. At one school, administrators would not allow the students to focus on women's rights or LGBTQ issues, even though the students selected them as areas they wanted to focus on. After involving the principal through interviews and discussions for action plans, the principal did allow women's rights to be dealt with, but the team decided to keep LGBTQ issues off the table for now. While the students themselves seem to be willing to focus on these issues, and there are several out students at that school, the community at large is very conservative. In order to be allowed the autonomy to do this curriculum, the teachers opted to self-censor in this particular area.

It is critical to take issues like this into account. The project itself is very rewarding for teachers and students alike, and it would be unfortunate if the entire curriculum was shut down over one issue. Of course, this is a decision that only you, and your team can make.

Issues that are difficult to find in novels—As students are living in contemporary society, there are issues that come up that are more recent and books have not necessarily been created that adequately address the issues in ways that work for your students. One potential solution is to do some of the pre-work about the issues they care about early in the semester or year you are planning to do this curriculum in order to have more time to search for books. This allows you to vet some of the novels prior to introducing them to your students, and you get to read some great novels for "work."

On occasion, you may find a reference that says a book focuses on one thing when, in fact, it only touches upon the issue in mild ways. Having that built-in time will help you discern those differences.

One group of students wanted to focus on net neutrality, or the government control of the internet, and the teachers were unable to identify young adult (YA) novels that addressed the issue. In order to allow the students to still stay somewhat focused on their issue, the teachers tried to get at what aspect of net neutrality did they find the most pressing. Was it the computer aspect, or was it the government control aspect?

In this case, the students ended up reading *Feed* by M. T. Anderson (2002), which is not about net neutrality at all, but does have an element of government control, which is what the students were most interested in exploring.

Purchasing the books—Once you have identified the books, the real fun begins.

- Amazon.com is a wonderful way to find multiple books.
- Book outlets might provide books at a discount, and sometimes publishers will provide multiple copies of books for a discounted price.
- You will want to provide enough copies for each person to read in their groups. Some teachers have asked their students to buy a copy of the book and then leave it in the classroom for other class periods to read.
- There are often small grants that might allow for the purchase of these novels.
- This is also where it would be beneficial to look into administrative support to develop a classroom library.

This initial cost is something that does diminish over time, as each successive year, you will have to buy fewer books. Many students are willing to donate their copies of the books to the classroom for future iterations.

STUDENT ACTIVITIES

The primary focus of these activities is to expose students to various social justice issues and have them consider their place within society. The ultimate goal will be for them to narrow their focus in order to begin the process of reading a novel for action.

Discussions of Privilege

There are multiple ways to help students understand their own privileges and realize what other individuals struggle with. This will be important depending upon the demographics of your students. Students who are relatively privileged will benefit from exploring the ways that they are able to maneuver through society more easily.

Privilege for Sale—While the concept of a privilege walk has become popularized by celebrities and viral videos, there may be some ethical concerns in asking students to self-identify as richer than, poorer than, and so forth. An alternative to this activity might be the following: you might open up the opportunity to discuss privilege and how different things that some people might take for granted are actually privileges.

While the director of the Social Justice Toolbox has detailed this activity on her site included in the resource link, here is a brief overview of the activity. Summarily, you will group the students into three to five members each, and give them an amount of money that varies from group to group along with a list of privileges. The groups must decide collectively which privileges they would purchase at $100.00 each.

This forces students to consider what they might already have in real life, and what types of advantages/disadvantages individuals might have. You can also tailor the list of privileges to your particular group of students in terms of what they may or may not already have. The varying budgets also help drive home the lack of control individuals might have over this issue.

Philosophical Chairs

Philosophical chairs is a way to encourage discussion about complex issues and to allow students to see that there are multiple ways to think about various issues. Immigration, for example, is a sticky topic without an easily agreed-upon solution to past events nor approach moving forward.

In order for students to participate in philosophical chairs, set up the classroom with an Agree side, a neutral space, and a Disagree side. Write a statement on the board that students might agree or disagree with, such as, America should provide immigrants with an easier path for citizenship. Students would then conduct research to support or disagree with this statement. After doing research, they would pick a side to stand on, and at that point, a representative from each side would use their research to attempt to persuade the other person to join their side.

This discussion prompts researched, critical thinking while also allowing students to see the complexities of a variety of social issues. The goal of this activity is not to dissuade students from choosing the topic they want to study, but instead to help them think about complex aspects of the problem in different ways so that when they are ultimately tasked with taking action, they will have some in-depth understanding of different ways to think about the issue. For more details about the philosophical chairs, see the resources table at the end of this section.

Brainstorming Issues

After students have been exposed to the nonfiction articles, they will be asked to brainstorm issues they might be interested in focusing on. At this point, they can really explore anything they are interested in, and the class will distill the myriad issues into a smaller group. Encourage the students to feel free to discuss multiple ideas here, as it is brainstorming and not a commitment to focus.

Social Identity Wheel

This social identity wheel allows students to recognize the ways that they have multiple identities. The wheel is a circle with various descriptors around it where students can indicate to what degree each concept has an effect on the way they perceive themselves, or how others perceive them. There is a link to a sample wheel activity found in table 3.3.

- Students are asked to rank a variety of categories with
  - 1 (identities you think about *most* often),
  - 2 (identities you think about *least* often),
  - 3 (your own identities you would like to learn more about),
  - 4 (identities that have the strongest effect on how you perceive *yourself*), and
  - 5 (identities that have the greatest effect on how *others* perceive you).

- Each category might have multiple numbers in the space, as a student might think about race most often, want to learn more about their race, and believe that race has the greatest effect on how others perceive them, for example.
- Some students may give no thought to these items at all, and it is okay for this to be the case. This may be an indicator that they are a member of the majority group in that particular category, which is something for students to think about as they work through the exercise.

As you facilitate the activity, you may need to provide support with the terminology. The terms students will be responding to are as follows:

- *Socioeconomic Status*—When students consider their personal and familial finances, it might be helpful to have them consider how their current status impacts their own behaviors or thoughts as they move through their community. For example, older students may have different thoughts about their future career or college path depending upon their financial resources. Younger students may have different definitions of what it means to be well-off as indicated by the types of things they would buy if they could.
- *Gender*—Gender is typically thought of in terms of societal roles. This may include the expectations that people have in terms of how people should dress or act, or what types of toys they play with. It might be good to talk about the role that gender expectations play in our decisions to help students think about how much this impacts their sense of identity.
- *Sex*—Sex refers to the biological differences between males and females. While there may be some overlap with gender, there are some nuanced differences between the two, and some individuals will have different reactions to each idea.
- *Sexual Orientation/Romantic Attraction*—Sexual orientation is defined as a person's identity in relation to the gender to which they are attracted. People may be heterosexual (attracted to the opposite gender), gay or lesbian (attracted to the same gender), bisexual (attracted to both genders), or asexual (attracted to neither). There are multiple other more nuanced categories for this area, although the primary goal of this wheel is to help students see that there are multiple facets to their sense of identity, and it may not be necessary to delve into all categories for all students. Older students may be more interested in discussing this in depth, and it may be advantageous to allow the opportunity to discuss the broadening scope of orientation for informational purposes. If you are in a more conservative area, or are teaching younger students, romantic attraction may be less inflammatory or touchy. https://www.refinery29.com/en-us/sexual-orientation-types-of-sexualities.

- *National Origin*—This is defined as the nation from which a person originates. So if someone is born in Mexico, but has become a citizen of the United States, their national origin is Mexico. If someone is born in America, their national origin is America, even if their family may have come from another country.
- *First Language*—First language refers to the language the student first learned to speak. While this may be English for many of your students, those who were raised in homes where English was not the predominant language may have a different relationship with this. How it impacts each individual will vary widely from person to person.
- *Physical, Emotional, Developmental (Dis)Ability*—This will include visible and nonvisible characteristics for individuals. While disability is defined as a disadvantage or handicap, especially one recognized by the law, it may be important to discuss the ability aspect of this category as well, such as gifted education. Additionally, some students may see diagnosed issues as abilities as opposed to disabilities, which can be important to discuss.
- *Age*—Many students are unable to move freely throughout their community due to assumptions made about their age. Some will feel this more acutely than others.
- *Religious or Spiritual Affiliation*—This may also refer to those students who are not religiously affiliated in a highly religious community.
- *Race*—Race is typically determined by physical characteristics which result from genetic ancestry. While there are actually very few scientifically genetic differences in humans, society has labeled some of those genetic differences as race, as opposed to simply characteristics.
- *Ethnicity*—Ethnicity refers to the person's identity in relation to a social, cultural, or religious group. This can be adopted by the individual, so it could potentially change depending upon the individual. For example, a person may convert to Catholicism and identify their ethnicity as Catholic from that point forward.

The original document and framing material can be found through the University of Michigan website focused on inclusive teaching. This resource and others mentioned above can be found in table 1.3.

PUTTING THEORY INTO PRACTICE

A suburban tenth grade honors course that followed this curriculum focused predominantly on the idea of identities and intersectionality in the beginning, as the students seemed fairly aware of the issues they were interested in focusing upon. The teacher, Ms. Neff, was more interested in making sure

Table 1.3 Teaching Activity Resources

Link to inequality article	https://webcache.googleusercontent.com/search?q=cache:WPmQojd-hFcJ:https://opinionator.blogs.nytimes.com/author/elizabeth-anderson/+&cd=1&hl=en&ct=clnk&gl=us&client=safari
Privilege for sale details	http://www.socialjusticetoolbox.com/activity/privilege-for-sale/
Philosophical chairs link	https://www.scholastic.com/teachers/lesson-plans/teaching-content/philosophical-chairs-discussion/
Social Identity Wheel	https://sites.lsa.umich.edu/inclusive-teaching/wp-content/uploads/sites/355/2018/12/Social-Identity-Wheel-3-2.pdf

that the students were open to seeing things from a different perspective. Because of this, she spent more time getting them to analyze their own privilege and preparing them to see different realities from their own.

The seventh grade teaching team spent more time exposing students to various issues. They did this through a variety of brainstorming techniques because their thought process was that students might not be as socially aware as they needed to be to begin this work.

Successes

The seventh grade team discovered that there were common threads across the grade levels for issues that needed to be addressed. Additionally, when they asked the students to consider what their concerns were for the school and community, it gave them insight into the issues that the students faced. Through their conversations, they discovered that bullying, drugs, and suicide were at the top of their list. Additionally, LGBTQ issues came up. This is important to note, because often seventh grade is seen as a more naïve or innocent time, but it turned out that the students were much more aware of difficult issues than the teachers previously realized.

One of the seventh grade teachers, Mr. Flores, utilized Adichie's "Danger of a Single Story" TED Talk video as a means of helping his students understand that there may be more than one narrative around an issue. He also talked to them about the reasons Jarrett Krosoczka wrote *Hey Kiddo* (2018). Mr. Flores stated that the students really began to understand each situation that was discussed and often identified with the stories they heard. For example, he had several students living with their grandparents, as the character in *Hey Kiddo* does, which created a stronger sense of empathy.

The tenth grade class began with Adichie's talk and discussed the multiple layers to the issues. They also completed a smaller, but similar project on bullying, in terms of conducting research and presenting solutions. Bullying was a critical issue at her school, both in person and through social media.

Ms. Neff found it very helpful to connect everything back to the idea of "The Danger of a Single Story," and eventually students began making their own connections between what they were reading and the ideas of the talk. Additionally, students were able to work on a similar project on a smaller scale before beginning the larger, more individualized project, which supported their end goals.

Struggles

Students who were absent from the frontloading of the material did not necessarily have the same emotional approach or connection to the issues, which was somewhat problematic. The tenth graders also seemed to be less prepared for the final project if they had not walked through the bullying project done as a class. Ms. Neff did introduce this unit at the beginning of the school year so students who transferred into the classes later, due to scheduling issues, were the ones who did not get all of the frontloading.

An additional issue that was difficult was trying to remain as neutral as possible while discussing the issues so that students could ultimately come to their own thoughts. If students have not been exposed to an issue, or conversely, have very strong opinions about the issue, there may be discussion or comments made that could inadvertently sway a class member. Beginning with the idea that there is always more than one side to any story seemed to help combat some of that.

The seventh graders were also inclined to want to choose what the teachers thought was important, and the teachers wanted to be sure that the students chose something they themselves cared about. This can be more difficult with lower grade levels, or with students who feel that in order to be successful, they must exhibit behaviors that their teacher likes to see. It will be critical for the educators to allow students to choose something they are passionate about in order for the project to truly work, so it will be important to try to keep from being overly passionate about one issue over another in order to let students see that their interests are enough.

CONCLUSION

Students often believe that what they do inside their classroom and what happens out in "the real world" are not necessarily interconnected. This work helps to build that bridge between these worlds and may ultimately increase student engagement in the classroom. Supporting students by valuing and honoring their thoughts on what should be explored and studied allows students to have buy-in to their own education, inherently making your job as an educator much easier. Additionally, developing students' capacity for civic engagement is a critical aspect of our democratic society. Adolescents who feel as though they have something to offer the broader social order may be more inclined to feel their classes are offering value to their educational career. This sense of connection with humanity may also increase prosocial behavior from students.

Chapter 2

Reading the Novels

"Mrs. Hays, why does every book we read have to be one where the main character dies?" This question should make every teacher pause. Let's reflect on the plot structure of many of our required texts, which include *To Kill a Mockingbird*, *The Great Gatsby*, *Of Mice and Men*, and *The Crucible* to name a few, and yes, death is typically the final plot twist. Miller's (2004) *NY Times* article, "Why Teachers Love Depressing Books" discussed the morbid reading choices of ELA teachers and our seeming need to drive the innocence out of our students, if you need further proof that our curriculum choices tend toward the morbid.

Counter to this argument is the idea that young adults deal with stark realities already, and contemporary novels that address these issues, yet also end on a note of hope, may actually be a lifeline for many of our students. Choosing novels for students to read is a heavy responsibility for educators: we must both ensure that the books demonstrate the quality of writing that we want our students exposed to, and consider the potential for engaging students.

For this curriculum to achieve its goals, it is important that the students get to focus on the social justice issue that they identified as their first or second choice. Providing choice to students has been shown to increase intrinsic motivation, which is critical for the reading to work smoothly and effectively (Patall et al. 2008). Intrinsic motivation is essential when students are struggling through a particularly tough passage or encounter writing that seems irrelevant to them on its surface.

Your students are unlikely to want to focus on the same issue; therefore, it is beneficial to ensure that your reading instruction is able to encompass multiple foci. One introductory approach that can be used over several grade levels is that of literature circles, initially developed by Harvey Daniels

(Daniels 2006; McElvain 2010; Brabham and Villaume 2000). As a side note, Daniels has spoken out against using these roles in every instance of small group reading, as they were intended to be a scaffold to help students see how readers think, as opposed to the only way to discuss a book (Daniels 2006).

Literature circles provide a framework for students to read novels in small, independent groups by guiding students through different types of textual analysis and reflection. There are multiple forms of literature circles, and a quick Google search will send you in a wide variety of directions and provide you with plenty of feedback and information that you can modify as you see fit. Later in this chapter you will find explanations of the most common literature circle roles.

Reading is the hallmark of English classes, and as reading for pleasure continues to drop throughout the country, reading engaging novels in our classrooms while we have some ability to influence students' reading diets may be our only hope. Too few students leave high school excited about reading, but this approach just might have an opportunity to change this attitude. This chapter aims to support you and your students in alternative ways to approach reading a novel that provides flexibility in topic, while still providing some structure. Refer to table 2.1 for an overview of activities.

WHAT THE TEACHER DOES

Before you begin with the literature circles, you must do some groundwork so your students can be successful within their groups.

Creating Groups

Using your brainstorming topic list, you will want to create groups that have no less than three, and no more than five members. If you have less than three students, they will be unable to hold conversations that offer any depth of perspective. If there are more than five students in a group, they tend to become more easily distracted and students are less likely to use the discussion

Table 2.1 Activity Overview

Teacher Does	Students Do
Organize groups	Participate in Literature Circles
Copy literature circle packets	
Develop a Reading Timeline	Take Collaborative notes
	Keep a journal while reading

opportunities in a realistic or authentic way. Additionally, this curriculum does require meeting outside of class typically, so four may be an optimal number for cooperative purposes.

Group discussion is critical because students who are given the opportunity to discover their own meaning in literature are more successful and motivated for future literacy activities than students who are guided more explicitly (Applebee et al. 2003; Moley et al. 2011). Having students who are all interested in the same topic will help with this, along with keeping the number of students per group four or five.

Setting up a Reading Timeline

You must also decide if you want to establish a reading calendar or if you want the students to divide the texts up on their own. If you are going to provide the reading calendar for them, you'll want to consider the book's length and reading levels. The amount of time that you provide will depend upon students' access to books, their reading levels, and how much time you plan for them to talk versus read during the period you have. Providing in-class reading time ensures that all students can complete the reading using the classroom set of books, whether or not they have access to the books outside the classroom.

To develop the reading calendar, divide each novel into as many equal parts as you have days to read in class. This does mean that some students will have to read more pages than others, although the level of writing in each book may negate the added length for the groups. Often some students tend to get through the books slightly faster than the educators expect them to, based upon previous experience at dragging students through some canonical, required class texts. While some people may feel that YA is an easier read, it is more likely that the students' engagement level is driving their appetite. In the next section, you'll find options you might use to keep those students engaged if they do finish faster than expected.

THINKING THROUGH IT

Consider Reading Attitudes

You'll need to consider the reading attitude of the students within each group. Their reading attitude may impact their choice of novel, as well as the group you consider assigning the students to. Donalyn Miller (2012) advocates for providing choices for students, as engagement will help students get through books. For example, if you have a large number of students who choose a particular issue, and half of them would not self-identify as readers, it may be advantageous to give them several different books, allow them to peruse them, and assign them different novels focused on the same issue as opposed to assigning everyone to the same novel. You might suggest that students look at the front cover, back cover, and the first page. If it seems interesting and accessible to them, that could be a good fit.

Do not assign a student to an issue they did not choose simply to give them an easier read! If students are not able to focus on the issue they are interested in, the independent work that makes this curriculum viable may not be as effective. You will also need to consider whether you only have a class set of books, or enough books so that each student can take one home. If students have the ability or desire to read at home, the reading may go faster.

Prepare Literature Circle Packets

You will also need to make copies of the literature circles packet that you choose to use. The students will change roles each day as described below, and the typical literature circle packet tends to have about six different roles. If you know that you have more than six days of reading scheduled, and you want them to remain accountable through these roles while in their discussion groups, you may decide to make extra copies of specific roles so students might repeat the role as a lead in one of the specific areas.

As there are also multiple variations of literature circle packets and worksheets, you could create your own combination of roles that you want to utilize within your classroom. You might also supplement the literature circle packets with alternate activities as discussed below.

STUDENT ACTIVITIES

Literature Circles

Before the students begin reading, they choose their first role from the literature circle packet that you choose to implement. For each subsequent discussion focused day, the students rotate roles, and by the end of the novel-reading portion, each student will have held every role at least once throughout the process.

While the individual roles allow for accountability, the discussion may not be as rich as you'd like, so previous teachers have asked the students to record their discussions on their smartphones and have had them upload their audio files to a digital folder that the teacher has access to. If this is an option for you and your students, this may add another layer of accountability into the process. The literature circles that have been used successfully include the following roles:

- Summarizer: This person provides a brief summary of the reading that had to be done for the class period, and leads the group discussion. The summary should include the key point, main highlights, and the general idea of the reading assignment.
- Discussion Director: This person develops a list of questions that the group might want to discuss about that section of the book. The goal is not to develop "right or wrong" or "yes or no" questions that can be easily found in the text, but ideas that might generate talk about connections with the book, and so on.
- Connector: This person tries to find connections between the book the group is reading and the world outside. This works quite well with this topic typically, because students will be required to conduct research for the second portion of this curriculum.
- Vocabulary Enricher: This person is on the lookout for important words in the reading. It is always fascinating to see how students take this up. They typically identify words that convey meaning to them, often moving beyond unfamiliar words.
- Investigator: This person's job is to dig up some background information on any topic related to the book. The list includes geography, weather, culture, or history of the book; the author; the time period portrayed; pictures, objects, or materials that illustrate elements of the book; the history and derivation of words or names used in the book; and music that reflects the book or its time.
- Illustrator: This person provides a visual depiction of the story in whatever form deemed appropriate. The visuals might be a literal interpretation of the setting of the story, or the characters, but it may also be an abstract depiction of events that are occurring. If the student is not a strong artist, you might allow them to find appropriate visuals online to alleviate any undue stress. This activity does work quite well for students who work more strongly in different modalities beyond writing.
- Travel Tracer: If appropriate to the book, this person tracks where the characters are at any given time throughout the novel. They also track how settings might have changed throughout the novel. This role works easily with a novel like *The Good Braider* by Terry Farish, which deals with a refugee fleeing her country, although students may struggle a bit more if the setting is more static.

Rotating through these roles gives each student an opportunity to practice seeing the novel through all six or seven perspectives. For each role, the packet includes writing or other materials that must be completed. Students should fill out their individual role before each small group discussion, so they can actively participate in those meetings. This also provides a measure of accountability for themselves, their peers, and the teacher. Additionally, the students may refer back to their literature circle packets as they complete the other aspects of the curriculum.

Collaborative Note Taking

If you have students who are more intrinsically motivated and driven, you may be able to provide less structure. Collaborative note-taking (Griffith 2017) is another method that provides you with a virtual check in for the students but requires less structured guidance than literature circles. As Griffith explains, collaborative note-taking can be done through Google Docs, and a list of categories can be created that each student can contribute to throughout their reading. This information can later be used to support any research work done through the project, or any subsequent action that might be taken.

It may be of use to do this work in tandem with the literature circles as a means of providing tangible, reflective evidence of the collective thought process as students begin to develop their action plans. Table 2.2 might be an example of what collaborative notes could look like.

Structured Identity Journal Entries

In addition to the group literature circles or collaborative note-taking, individual student journals provide an opportunity to keep a written record of ongoing thinking and self-reflection. Students may have the option of simply reflecting on their own experience throughout the book, or they may benefit from more guided questions. Since the final project asks the students to generate an action plan to solve the issue, it is important for them to immerse

Table 2.2 Collaborative Notes Example

Chapter	Issues that Come Up	Vocabulary	Plot-Based Discussion Questions	Ideas to Take Action
14	Not being able to buy lunch Being made fun of for having the wrong clothes	Disdain (120) Distress (111)	When Eleanor decides to sit by the trash can, how is this perpetuating the attitude people might have toward her? Does her lack of trendy clothes make her nonsocial?	Clothing drive Reaching out to people who are alone at lunch

themselves in the issues, and the journaling allows them to reflect solely on their own thought process.

In order to promote student thinking about their identification with the characters as well as how they might ultimately take action, teachers asked students to respond to the following questions throughout the weeks that they spent reading. They were asked to complete a journal entry each day of the week, and they answered a modified version of those questions after each subsequent week. The questions in textbox 2.1 are those that were adapted by Ms. Neff in her third iteration of the curriculum.

TEXTBOX 2.1

Entry #1 Questions (to be completed by the end of week one)
What character do you most identify with so far? Why?
What emotions did you have during your reading yesterday? Why?
What part of the novel so far, is significant? Why?
How is this book portraying a social injustice so far?
What do you think of the novel so far?

Entry #2 Questions (to be completed by the end of week two)
Do you still identify with the same character you identified with last week? Why or why not? Explain.
What emotions did you have during this week's readings? Why?
What part of the novel so far, is significant to you personally? Why?
Has the novel's portrayal of a social injustice changed from your last journal entry? How so? Have any new social issues been brought up in the novel?
If you could create a new character to be in the novel, what would your new character be like? What would they do in the novel? Why?

Entry #3 Questions (to be completed by the end of week three)
How did this novel make you feel toward the character you most identified with? Why?
How do you feel about the social issue that took place in the novel? Did you relate to it? Did your perspective change at all on the social issue as a result of reading this novel?
If you could do anything to bring change and awareness to the social issue in the novel what would you do?
What about this novel was the most significant to you? Why?
Would you recommend this novel to your friends or family? Why or why not?

We asked questions about character because it is important for students to consider the humans involved in these social issues. Asking them to identify characters they related to, while also asking them to consider their own feelings toward the characters both before and after the reading, is an important step toward their sociocultural awareness and cognitive processing. This active recall of their feelings allows them to think through and identify their ideas in a more concrete fashion.

We asked the students what emotions they were having in order to ascertain whether they were experiencing feelings more akin to helplessness, or feelings that might lead to productive action. These emotions have the potential to transfer to their lived experiences with the issue.

We also asked the students to identify the areas of the novel they found significant with the hope that it might help them identify concepts that mattered in regard to addressing the issue they were focused on.

Finally, students were asked to write their ideas about how they might take action from a position of ultimate power so that their imaginations were not limited. Part of the goal of this project and this reading is to support students on their way to developing agency, and the imagination is a powerful component of that work. Additionally, allowing students to begin processing their thinking before taking action may help them avoid feeling adrift when they finish the book.

These journal entries can be completed online or on paper. While all of the teachers who have done this curriculum have one-to-one technology, in which each student has his or her own computing device, Ms. Neff, the tenth grade teacher, utilizes OneNote more regularly in her classroom and her students are very comfortable with being online throughout their school day. When students keep their journals in their OneNote accounts, she can check on their progress more often.

In addition, when she begins to conference with the students, she is able to pull from their own thinking as she advises them on their projects. She does provide students the option to write on paper if they are more comfortable doing that.

In contrast, the junior high teachers found using Google Chromebooks for journal completion to be somewhat burdensome, so they preferred to have the students complete these journal entries by hand in a composition notebook. The real value of these entries is the self-reflection that students are doing, and the ultimate brainstorming for their final project, so please do whichever works best for you and your students.

PUTTING THEORY INTO PRACTICE

Ms. Neff's suburban tenth grade honors course allocates approximately six days of class to focus specifically on reading the novel. The teacher,

Ms. Neff, gives the students three weeks in which to read their novel, complete the literature circle packet, and answer the journal prompts found below. She mandates that Tuesday and Thursday are in-class reading days, and the students may use the other three days of class in order to have their discussions, catch up on reading, or work on their journals. This works well because Tuesdays and Thursdays are less likely to be interrupted by school events or field trips, so the students are likely to have consistent access to the class sets of books.

While there were several students who did find copies of the books for themselves to read at home, she allocates in-class time for reading so students who cannot get their own books are not negatively affected. She allows the students to divide their books into appropriate chunks, instead of prescribing how much they should get through on each day. She changed to this strategy after realizing that many students were reading ahead or getting frustrated by the reading schedule's limitations. The student-driven timeline has not generated any organizational issues for her, and the increased student buy-in is an added benefit.

Three rural seventh grade classes taught by Mr. Muñoz, Mr. Frost, and Mr. Flores allocated approximately fifteen days of class to complete the reading, literature circles, and journals. The students read Tuesdays, Wednesdays, and Thursdays, and worked on literature circles and journals on Fridays. Mondays were allocated to school-wide reading instruction.

These teachers operate in a tightly knit Professional Learning Community (PLC) and regularly work together on pacing guides, and they chose to develop a reading calendar for their students. The rural setting of the town does not afford the students the same access to resources, so it is even more critical than the tenth grade class that students have time to finish the novels in class. While there were some students who read ahead, it was not as significant a number as the tenth grade honor students (table 2.3).

Successes

The successes of the students at this point of the curriculum can be found both in their engagement with the reading, with each other, and with their topics. Not all successes are academic in this case, but they are equally important.

Reading Engagement Increased

It may feel a bit daunting to imagine your students reading independently without the heavy guidance of the instructor as this is often contrary to the typical structure of an ELA classroom. However, the choice of a YA novel that deals with difficult yet realistic subject matter can provide students with

Table 2.3 Sample Calendar

Monday	Tuesday	Wednesday	Thursday	Friday
Get into Lit Circle Groups/ Assign roles/ Create Reading Calendar	In-class time for reading	Literature Circle Discussion #1/ Reading time	In-class time for reading	Literature Circle Discussion #2/ Journal response time
Monday Full-class discussion of project goals Nonfiction article to support connection with social issue and novel	**Tuesday** In-class time for reading	**Wednesday** Literature Circle Discussion #3/ Reading time	**Thursday** In-class time for reading	**Friday** Literature Circle Discussion #4/ Journal response time
Monday Full-class discussion of speaking skills	**Tuesday** In-class time for reading	**Wednesday** Literature Circle Discussion #5/ Reading time	**Thursday** In-class time for reading	**Friday** Literature Circle Discussion #6/ Journal response time

the engagement necessary to stay on task (G. Ivey and Johnston 2018) and literature circles can provide individualized guidance. In addition to enabling the teacher to release control within the classroom, there are many successes that Mr. Muñoz, Mr. Frost, Mr. Flores, and Ms. Neff have experienced as they have worked through this curriculum.

Students Connect

Since the students are working within their small groups, and are ultimately self-guided, they tend to connect with one another in more significant ways. The discussions in literature circles promote more participation from each individual in the group. It is much harder to shrink behind other voices when you are one of four or five, as opposed to one of thirty or even forty.

As Applebee (2003) wrote, discussion-based practices lend themselves to deeper levels of understanding. Through the conversations that students have, individual students realize that they have more in common with one another than they may have previously thought. This connection lends itself to a stronger classroom community, which ultimately results in more honest and thoughtful discussions for the full class. It may be in your best interest to open your school year with this project, as students will maintain this sense of community.

Students Relate

In addition to connecting with their group members, students also relate to the characters in the books, to people who they may not have seen a connection with earlier, and to other peers in the classroom. Throughout this work, there are often individuals who do not have prior experience with the issue that they chose.

As Jasmin, who read *Chinese Handcuffs* by Chris Crutcher, explained in her post-reading interview, "I never understood why people would ever do drugs, but I understand why people might think this was a good solution." She was talking, in this case, about characters who had experienced a significant level of abuse both physically and mentally, who were shown in the novel as drinking at a party.

Jasmin stated that she and her family have vowed to never drink or take any sort of mind-altering substance. She does not condone the moves that the characters make in the novel, but she did discuss that she could understand or empathize with them. This empathy is the first step in developing solutions for problems, and since Jasmin related to the characters in other ways, she was better able to put herself in their shoes.

Another student was able to relate to the refugee experience depicted in *The Good Braider* by Terry Farish and turned this sense of identity to the refugees that were being hosted by her church. While she already had a high level of empathy, her ability to see, through the story, that the character had similar feelings and aspirations to herself, she was able to consider useful ways to support refugees.

As students discover that their peers have similar experiences to themselves through the discussion, they develop a strong sense of relating to one another as well. For example, a group of relatively disparate students chose to read *The Circuit*, and through discussion during the literature circles, they discovered that all but one of them had begun kindergarten as a Spanish-only speaker, which resulted in a sense of connection between them.

Students Seek Out More

Part of this curriculum involves students conducting research on their issue, with the ultimate goal of generating an action plan that makes moves to address the issue in some way. One way that this reading supports that future work is by providing students with an accessible background narrative. Through reading the novel, the students are exposed to characters who are dealing with the issue they are interested in, and the novels offer them opportunities to see the issue from different perspectives.

These perspectives, which Bishop (1990) calls windows, have inspired our students to look for research that supports or contradicts the stories they are finding—sometimes from a place of disbelief that this could be reality, and sometimes to verify that this does in fact happen to "real" people in their own community. Often times, this research winds up in the group discussion, or in the presentations that students might do later. You, as the teacher, should prompt your students to begin seeking out more information as soon as possible.

Self-Contained

One of the most beneficial aspects of this reading approach is that the students' work is self-contained. While you must be present to facilitate the reading groups, and occasionally nudge students to stay on track, much of the work is done by the students themselves. If you have provided a strong enough structure for the literature circles, they will be able to walk into the classroom, get out their novels, get into their groups, and begin their work on their own. Your role becomes that of a facilitator and mentor as opposed to the stereotypical sage on the stage.

Peer-to-Peer Accountability

You may have experienced students being reluctant to read the class novel throughout your teaching career. (If you are like me, you may have struggled to get students engaged in the reading and tried punitive measures such as reading check quizzes, or reward systems much like Accelerated Reader programs, or even reading an entire novel aloud in hopes that it might stick.) The approach described in this chapter seems to eliminate at least some of that struggle for the teachers because the peers tend to hold one another accountable for the reading.

Book talks from peer to peer are far more effective than book recommendations from teachers, and this same collegial relationship seems to hold true for the reading as well. Additionally, a portion of the grade might be group-based, which can encourage some students to nudge their colleagues to complete the reading. For example, the literature circle packets and journal entries might be submitted individually, but the groups will usually present a book talk or mini-research project together, which is discussed in the next chapter.

Struggles

All of this is not to say that problems will not arise throughout the reading. With our larger than ever secondary classrooms, students will be at vastly differing reading levels and a variety of motivational levels. As such, there may be some problem solving that you may need to do involving pacing and comprehension.

Pacing

All teachers who have completed this curriculum have run into issues with students reading ahead of the schedule. Several approaches can help to keep students engaged even after they have finished the book. One option is to point students toward another novel that also addresses a similar issue. You might provide those in your classroom through a check-out system for the students who want to read more stories. Sending the students to the school or public library may also be a viable alternative if you are unable to purchase the books for your classroom.

Another option is to suggest that the students reread the novel. Second readings provide a more in-depth understanding of events in the novel, and may even bring to light previously missed material or aspects of the issue. Finally, you can have students begin working on the research or action plan portion of their project. This might include reading nonfiction articles about the issue that are based within their community, or it may include students reaching out to professionals within their community that do the work they are looking to do for their own action plan.

Staying on Track

While the YA novels are likely to be accessible to the students, there may still be issues with students who have difficulty getting through the novel. Mr. Muñoz discovered this with a group of students who read *Hoot* by Carl Hiaasen. While this particular novel is geared toward students who are ages nine to twelve, his twelve- or thirteen-year-old students struggled with the novel. This may be due to a lack of engagement with the topic, although the teacher believed it may also have been due to their general struggles with reading comprehension.

To alleviate this, Mr. Muñoz obtained the audio version of the book and allowed students to listen to the recording while following along in their book. This ensured that the students were able to get the content from the book and were still exposed to the ways that the social issue might manifest itself in various ways.

In order to make sure that this happens appropriately, it will be important to assess the reading attitudes of the groups once you have sorted through their topic choices and possibly choose books that also offer an audio version. Many libraries offer audiobooks as part of their services, so you may be able to access these resources for free.

Another consideration in choosing the novels for your groups is that the exposure to the stories and varied aspects of the social issue is far more important than Lexile levels or difficulty levels. If you have students who struggle with reading comprehension in a group, it might be useful to consider implementing text sets (Pytash et al. 2014) in order to provide a variety of materials to support understanding of the concept. Alternatively, the literature circle group discussions help with ensuring that students who are part of heterogeneous groups are grasping the material throughout the process, so if the reading levels are widely mixed, it may be okay to challenge some students so long as you feel they will have the support necessary to grasp the material, and hopefully become inspired to struggle through the reading.

CONCLUSION

There are several options that you have during the reading for this unit, but you are required to keep several things in mind:

First, students must be allowed to read a novel that is focused on the issue they are interested in studying. If they are asked to read something on an issue they did not choose, they may not have a strong interest in the novel, and without that interest, this independent work may not be as effective.

Second, the books themselves must be engaging YA novels for your particular students. The appendix provides brief descriptions of several novels that address social justice issues. You should choose novels that you think your particular students would find intriguing that address the issues they have chosen, or better yet, ask your students to help you choose.

Finally, the most important aspect of the reading is that the students develop some connection with the characters in the books they read so that they have the potential for higher levels of intrinsic motivation to solve the issue discussed. Even if they do not personally identify with the characters as being like them and if they have developed a sense of empathy through the study of the character's story (Alsup 2015), they will be more likely to see the need to take action.

Additionally, if students already have a deep sense of empathy due to their own life experiences, seeing the story through the lens of taking action may increase levels of agency so that they feel more capable of making change. As such, it is critical that the students be afforded the opportunity to experience the books in as authentic a way as possible, which provides for a deeper reading experience.

Chapter 3

Building Capacity and Engaging Community

"Why do we even have to do research? All we're doing is writing down someone else's words, and not even doing anything."

"Well, you can just find a completed research paper online if you really want one."

Obviously, these students did not see the ultimate purpose of completing the senior research project in the same way the curriculum designer did, if this is how they were talking about it.

If you have ever seen a fan try to find information about their favorite YouTuber, it is clear that adolescents have research skills. They are willing to look at multiple sources of information, and they will collaborate with others to share information. This is what a researcher does, and the goal is to share that understanding with students, while simultaneously meeting the current call to support students becoming critical readers and consumers of information (R. E. Probst 2017).

While research in classrooms is often presented as looking up, reading, and synthesizing other people's words, it ought to be more than this. When students are engaged in a research project they are personally invested in, and if they are given the tools to conduct original inquiry, they can develop a sense of agency and purpose. This inquiry allows students to see themselves as researchers, even if they may not call themselves that (Hurst 2015). The goal of this chapter is to give you tools for creating a stronger sense of purpose so that students might feel more engaged with their research.

This curriculum's inquiry stance is that students ought to be trying to find out information in order to get at a potential solution to a problem, as opposed to reporting back to someone else. This approach to research can support students in moving beyond the regurgitation of facts so often produced by students on typical research products.

Table 3.1 Activity Overview

Teacher Does	Students Do
Support students in narrowing their topic	Write questions that come up while reading
	Fill out problem tree graphic organizer
Introduce students to both primary and secondary research sources	Conduct and annotate secondary research
	Conduct primary research through identifying stakeholders
Teach students professional email writing	Create and send email to various stakeholders
	Conduct interviews
Teach student professional speaking/presenting	Prepare presentation on their research to share with their peers

This chapter will detail the steps that teachers might take to actualize the content students are reading about in their novels by narrowing their research topic and conducting a variety of research activities. An overview of the activities can be found in table 3.1. In addition, several helpful resource links are provided in table 3.3 at the end of this chapter.

WHAT THE TEACHER DOES

In order to prepare students to conduct productive and thoughtful research, you can begin by helping students identify and focus their research questions. Next, to help students plan their research steps, you should prepare them to understand the difference between secondary research and primary research and aid them in identifying sources. Additionally, you will need to guide students toward making connections between their research and real-world events. Finally, you will want to make sure the students understand various ways to present that research.

Focusing the Research Question

Students need to understand that they are conducting research in order to ultimately answer a question, and they will need help with narrowing down what they really are interested in researching. When the students brainstormed their issues, they probably came up with broad, sweeping topics, like racism, gender equality, or poverty. While these are helpful in a general sense, they don't necessarily lead them down a fruitful research path.

There are a couple of different ways that students can narrow their focus. One way would be through tracking their thoughts and questions during the novel reading. If you encourage students to take notes or journal questions about extraneous topics that arise as they read, this will be much more useful for them when they embark upon the research process. They might notice the smaller, secondary issues that surround the "big picture" issue of their topic, which can be more useful to research when it comes time to think about steps they can take.

It is likely that the novel may end up taking them in a slightly different direction than anyone expected. For example, one group of students who read *The Circuit* (Jimenez 1997) ended up focusing on English Language Learners' instruction in school as opposed to the topic of immigration, which they had originally chosen. This research arose from the issues that the protagonist dealt with in the novel. Additionally, it was something that the students identified with, and ultimately felt they could act upon, while immigration in its entirety seemed overwhelming.

A second way to narrow the research topic is by reading one to two related nonfiction articles and taking notes to see what comes up for them. For example, if they have chosen poverty, they may end up finding an article that focuses specifically on poverty within a smaller subset of the population that they find really interesting. Encourage them to follow their hearts in this way. If they do that, they are more likely to enjoy what they are researching and go even further than they may have gone before.

Additionally, the Problem Tree activity (discussed in the Student Activities section later) can support students as they narrow their topics. This visual organizer will meet the needs of different learners, and may also allow students to see multiple approaches to a very complex and nuanced issue.

Understanding and Identifying Research Sources

While many students have conducted research in schools, it has most likely been some form of historical research. This may mean that much of their knowledge is around secondary sources. Since you will be asking them to take action, they may find it important and useful to also conduct primary research.

- *Secondary Research*—Many students are naturally inclined to turn to Google or some other public access research engine. You can help students understand the difference between evidence-based writing and opinion writing, and how to identify useful, relevant keywords to use in their research. It is important that the students learn how to find information that has already been vetted for credibility.

    The best tool for students to conduct their research would be library databases. If you are lucky enough to have a school librarian, they are quite helpful, and typically are willing to spend a class period or two teaching students how to search the library databases. If you do not have a school librarian, there are multiple websites and library guides available online. One of these can be found in the resources table at the end of the chapter.

Students will probably ask how many resources they need to have for their final project. As the goal is to make sure that students have a strong, well-rounded understanding of the topic, they should probably have five different sources at minimum. It may also be helpful to give them specific types of resources you will accept, such as, two peer-reviewed research articles, one government website, and two others. (The other might include videos, news clips, newspaper resources, websites, etc.). In order to validate the information they are finding, it is important that they find their facts in a variety of places. See table 3.3 at the end of this chapter for a link to a helpful library search guide and a link to a guide on annotating articles.
- *Primary Research*—Since the research topics for this project should be community based, some or much of the students' research should come from primary sources. This means that the experiences and information are coming directly from someone's mouth, as opposed to reading it "second-hand" in an article, for example. You will want to help students identify members of the community that can help with this.

Suggestions might include local university professors/researchers who have some firsthand knowledge, activists who are working to change the issue within the community, students and teachers on your campus, or even people spread out around the state who are doing the work they are interested in. You will want to help the students develop a script or email to reach out to these people and solicit their information. It will also be useful and important to develop a set of interview questions to ask those individuals so that they might get more useful responses.

Making Connections

One important goal of this curriculum is to help students see the reality of issues they are discovering within their novel in their present-day life. One great way to do this is by incorporating nonfiction articles into their literature circles or readings. The *New York Times* has a wonderful set of resources that often support the topics students choose. National Public Radio (NPR) also covers serious issues quite often throughout their daily programming, and their material is accessible through npr.org. This will require that students have access to streaming internet, as well as headphones in order to avoid a cacophony of noise if you are doing this work in the classroom!

Sharing Information

You will want to allow for space within the curriculum so students can share their work with others. This might be with their small groups, or to the class at large. Some individuals have even had students share their research with the entire school, which can be a useful way to make their writing more public, creating higher engagement and authenticity (Graham and Perin 2007).

There are several ways to have them share this work, and you might have them do this as individuals, or as groups.

- The first share might include preliminary research in the form of a stock secondary source presentation. This is when the students give the base facts about the issue, its causes and effects, and perhaps an overview of stakeholders. If you have students who want to switch topics when it comes time to take action, these presentations might help.
- The second share might include the action plan. Students can share either their ideas about how they might take action on this issue or if you are fortunate enough to have them commit to taking action, they might share the results of their moves at this point.

The rubric for evaluating student presentations should include both content-oriented and presentation-oriented material. Table 3.2 is a rubric you might utilize for this presentation.

STUDENT ACTIVITIES

The students will need to be led through activities that help them begin to think like researchers trying to solve a problem as opposed to simply looking up information to report out. Part of this work will include having students identify the complex aspects of the issue, as well as thinking through who the stakeholders are. Ultimately, they will need to be empowered to reach out to those stakeholders and think of themselves as collaborators in solving these problems on some small level.

Preresearch Activities

Knowing where to begin with research is often the most difficult task for many of us. The following activities will help students begin to isolate the focus they might be interested in exploring.

Table 3.2: Oral Presentation Rubric

	4–Excellent	3–Good	2–Fair	1–Needs Improvement
Delivery	-Holds attention of entire audience with the use of direct eye contact, seldom looking at notes -Speaks with fluctuation in volume and inflection to maintain audience interest and emphasize key points	-Consistent use of direct eye contact with audience, but still returns to notes -Speaks with satisfactory variation of volume and inflection	-Displays minimal eye contact with audience, while reading mostly from the notes -Speaks in uneven volume with little or no inflection	-Holds no eye contact with audience, as entire report is read from notes -Speaks in low volume or monotonous tone, which causes audience to disengage
Content/ Organization	-Demonstrates full knowledge by answering all-class questions with explanations and elaboration -Provides clear purpose and subject; pertinent examples, facts, or statistics; supports conclusions/ideas with evidence	-Is at ease with expected answers to all questions, without elaboration -Has somewhat clear purpose and subject; some examples, facts, or statistics that support the subject; includes some data or evidence that supports conclusions	-Is uncomfortable with information and is able to answer only rudimentary questions -Attempts to define purpose and subject; provides weak examples, facts, or statistics, which do not adequately support the subject; includes very thin data or evidence	-Does not have a grasp of information and cannot answer questions about subject -Does not clearly define subject and purpose; provides weak or no support of subject; gives insufficient support for ideas or conclusions
Enthusiasm/ Audience Awareness	-Demonstrates strong enthusiasm about topic during entire presentation -Significantly increases audience understanding and knowledge of topic; convinces an audience to recognize the validity and importance of the subject	-Shows some enthusiastic feelings about topic -Raises audience understanding and awareness of most points	-Shows little or mixed feelings about the topic being presented -Raises audience understanding and knowledge of some points	-Fails to increase audience understanding of knowledge of topic -Shows no interest in topic presented

Journal Writing—As students are reading, you might have them complete the following thinking stems at the end of each chunk they read, or at the end of lit circle meeting. This might give them something more manageable to think about when they begin researching the actual topic.

- I wonder . . .
- I notice . . .
- I think . . .

Problem Tree—This activity allows students to spend some time brainstorming and thinking through the complex aspects that their issue might have, as very rarely are social problems easily solved. For this activity, provide the students with the outline of a tree, or have the students draw a tree. You can find an example in figure 3.1.

- The center of the tree: The trunk of the tree is the core problem itself. While students may be able to start with this, as they continue working on the causes and effects of the issue, they may realize that the core problem is actually somewhat different than they initially thought.
- The roots of the tree: The roots of the tree are the causes or the phenomena that led to the problem. You can ask students to try to answer the question, "Why does this problem exist?" Another aspect to consider is the idea that one "Why" might lead to another "Why," which might lead to yet another "Why." Encourage the students to continue thinking about all of the various aspects of the problem that have roots in society.
- The leaves of the tree: The leaves of the tree are the effects of the issue. Encourage students to think about the myriad effects that could happen for each part of the issue. This imagery can help students understand that if they only try to address the effects of the problem, it is much like pruning a tree. The effects of the problem will come back quickly. One question that students can continue to ask until they've exhausted all of their options is "Then what happens?"

This problem tree activity might be done in several waves. Students could fill the tree out with information they have in their prior knowledge bank, and then work with partners or small groups, and finally fill it in with researched information. This will allow the students to develop a stronger understanding of the complexity of their issue as well as providing them multiple entry points to their final action plan by breaking the issue down into smaller parts. Refer to table 3.3 for a link to this resource (figures 3.1a and 3.1b).

Table 3.3 Teaching Resources

Library search guide:	https://library.northeastern.edu/get-help/research-tutorials/effective-database-searches/top-ten-search-tips
Guide to annotating an article:	http://www.readwritethink.org/files/resources/lesson_images/lesson1133/GuidetoAnnotating.pdf
Preparing effective presentations	http://www.orangeschools.org/PresentationGuidelines.aspx
Problem tree	https://cdn.we.org/wp-content/uploads/2016/05/Part-1-Activity_ProblemTree_May27.pdf
General presentation rubric	http://www.readwritethink.org/files/resources/printouts/30700_rubric.pdf

Secondary Research Activities

As part of the work they should do to make the connection between their novel and the world outside the classroom, they should read and annotate contemporary and scholarly articles focused on the issue. This will hit the nonfiction aspect of standards, while simultaneously providing relevance to your students and their project.

Nonfiction Articles—Students are quite adept at finding news articles online typically, although you may want to provide them with resources that you find to ensure factual information is being presented. If students are working in small groups, ask each of them to bring one news article that talks about their issue to class on a particular day. Encourage the students to try to find news articles from local community sources if possible, although it might also be interesting to have students compare their regional newspaper to a national publication to analyze tone and attitude toward the topic.

Many school libraries have a database that focuses specifically on news articles. NewsELA is also a great resource that allows teachers to assign articles to students, and the reading levels can be changed. The site does require a sign-in. As of 2021, educators can access current events for free, although genres outside of current events do require a subscription.

One way to potentially differentiate for students might be to have them search for podcasts or audio news bits. As discussed earlier, NPR.org archives all of their pieces, and often go into a fair amount of detail on issues that students may be interested in exploring. An additional advantage of utilizing NPR is their unlimited free access, whereas other sources may have a paywall. As students work through their nonfiction articles, they will want to take note of information that might support their future presentations or action plan.

Annotation—One way that they might note relevant information is through annotation of the articles. Essentially, annotation means underlining or

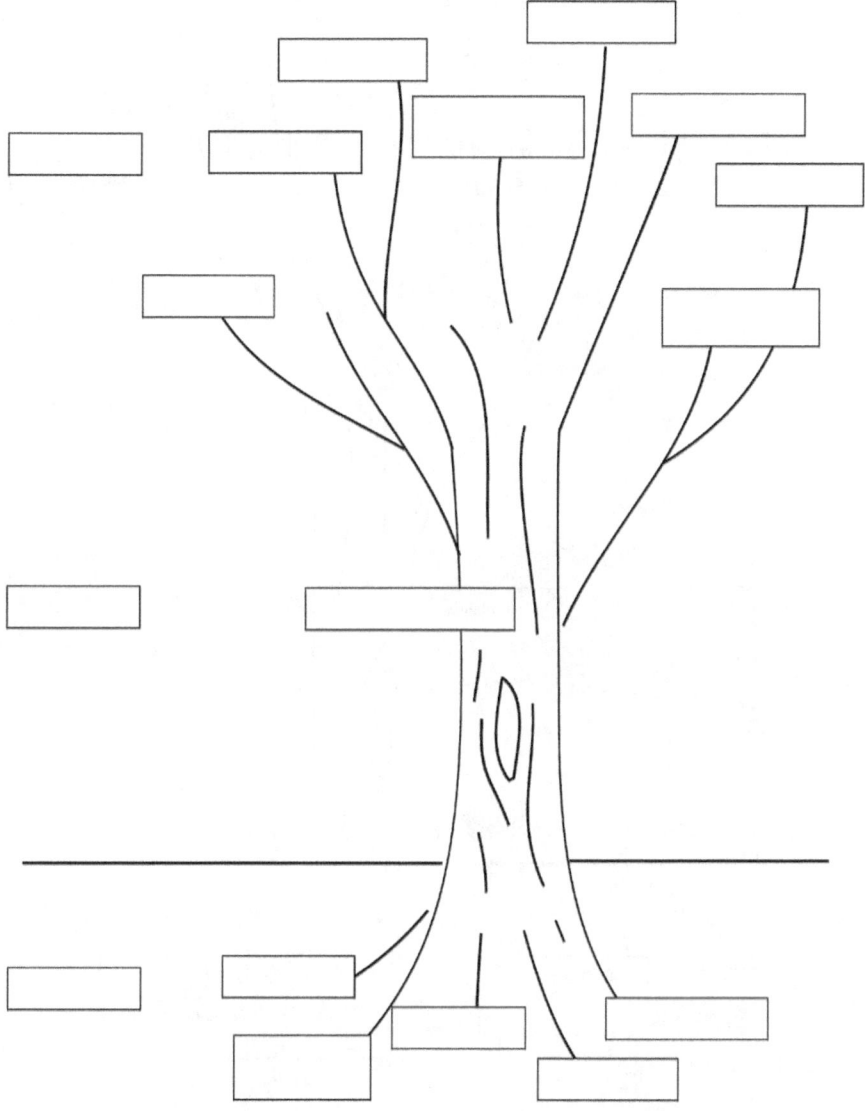

Figure 3.1a Problem Tree Template. *Source*: Eric Harper.

marking text in a way that helps the user understand the material. A well-annotated text will clearly identify where important ideas and information are located, express the main ideas of the text, trace the development of ideas or arguments in the text, and include some of the reader's thoughts and reflections as they are going through the article.

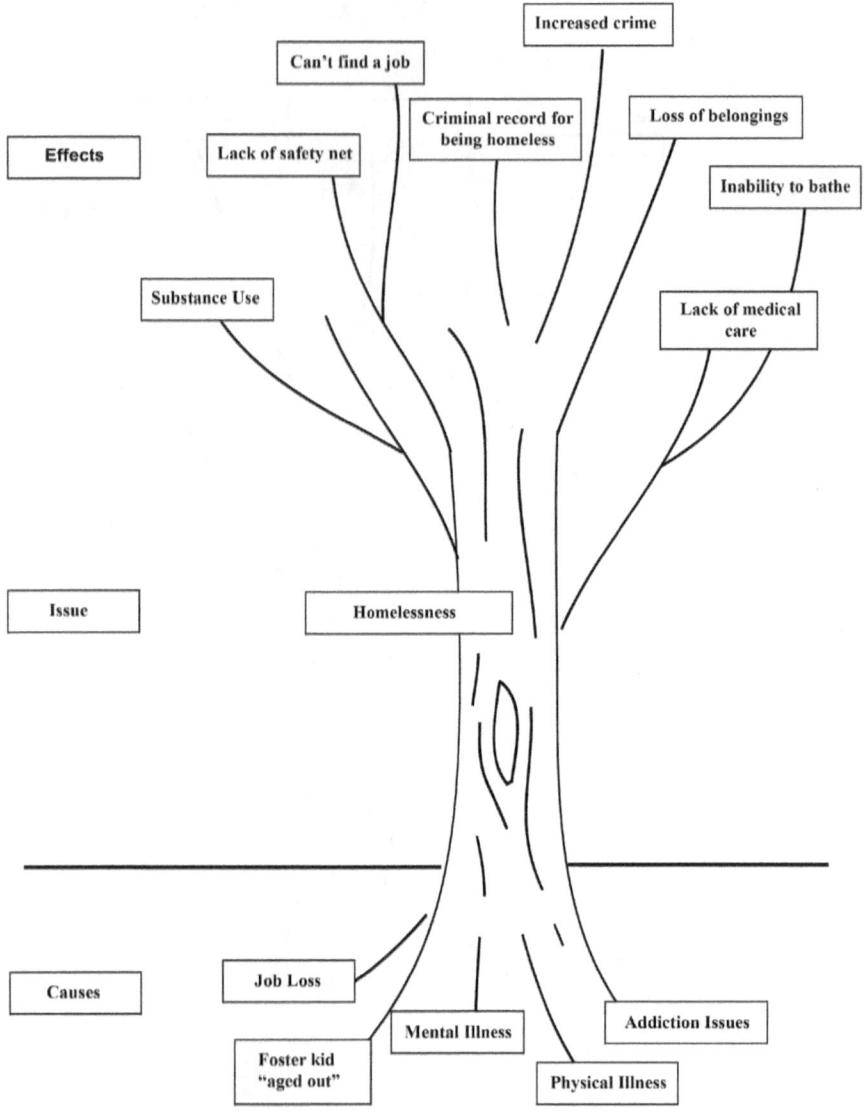

Figure 3.1b Problem Tree Example.

While there are a variety of ways to annotate, students should include the following basics:

1. Underline the main idea of the text.
2. Paraphrase or summarize the main idea at the end of the piece.
3. Identify aspects of the argument developed by the author including use of facts vs. opinion. (This may also be an opportunity to have

students identify the use of logos, pathos, and ethos if relevant to your standards.)
4. Include personal comments along the side that question the author's claims, help the reader remember what they were thinking at that moment, or identify potential causes and effects of the focus issue.
5. Identify organizations, individuals, or groups who are tackling the issue they are focused on.

The ultimate goal of learning annotation skills is to help students read for deeper understanding. Annotating has the additional benefit of providing fodder for students as they move into their action plans down the road. Further resources can be found in table 3.1.

Primary Research Activities

Primary research will often be a new skill or concept for your students. This allows students to research firsthand accounts surrounding the issue. Many history teachers focus on the use of primary documents, and this work can help students understand what exactly primary sources are.

Identifying Affected Stakeholders—It is critical that students get information from people in their surrounding area if the topic they chose impacts their local community. This means that they will need to interview individuals who have some stake (stakeholders) in the issue. This could include their parents, their friends, and the teachers in the community, among others.

The first thing they ought to do is brainstorm a list of people can think of who might have information that would help them understand how the issue impacts each of them. It will be important for them to think through the varied voices and positions that people have in order to get a fully developed sense of the issue as it presents itself within the community.

For example, if a student was focused on homelessness, it would be important to speak to both people in the specific community at large, as well as individuals who work in shelters and have more intimate knowledge of individuals who are homeless. Each of these people has information and insight about the issue from very different perspectives.

Identifying Potential Collaborator(s)—In addition to stakeholders directly affected by the issue, students will need to identify people who could potentially support an action plan to address the issue.

Students might do this by reaching out to local colleges or universities and finding individuals who study similar fields to the one they are interested in. They should also look to city, county, school district, or state legislative bodies and identify individuals who are championing or blocking legislation or other actions relevant to the areas that the student has identified as important.

If they have identified an issue that is educationally based, for example, they may want to reach out to the local school board. Identifying a minimum of five potential stakeholders is a good idea. (Many of these individuals are very busy, and may not be able to respond, but getting a response from someone in power can be transformative for students, so whatever can be done to make that happen is important.)

Developing Specific Questions—Students may not have experience in speaking to adults as collaborators, so it is important to help them think through specific questions they need to ask. This might be an opportunity for students to ask the stakeholders about their thoughts on actions that have already been taken. This will demonstrate to the outside adult that your students have done their research.

They may also use this as an opportunity to ask for suggestions about next steps. Sometimes these stakeholders have many ideas but are unable to act upon them due to their own swamped schedules. One student I know emailed the United Nations representative on Human Trafficking and simply asked what could be done at the school level and learned all about Amnesty International, which was an important outreach program to the ambassador.

Whichever way they go, it is important that the students do not simply tell the stakeholder that they are researching the topic in question and ask if they can help. There needs to be a clear request or call to action from the student to the stakeholder that the person can respond to if the student wants to increase their chances of finding support.

Outreach via Email—Email may be the best approach for the initial contact with some stakeholders and most potential collaborators. It can be used for scheduling in-person or phone interviews and, if these are not practical, for collecting answers to the students' questions. Make sure that the students can receive emails in response, particularly if they are utilizing a school email. Often times, they are not able to receive mail from outside contacts if they have a school-generated address, and this can be discouraging.

The following template in textbox 3.1 can serve as a guide for developing effective emails.

TEXTBOX 3.1 EMAIL TEMPLATE

To _____ (Specific name or title here, i.e., director of affairs).
Subject _____ (Specific area we have chosen to focus on.)

We would be very much interested in speaking with you about your work. [If they are a professor, maybe say research; if they are a legislator, maybe say policies.] If possible, could we schedule a time to talk on the phone or in person?

If that does not work, would you be able to answer the following questions that we have? [At this point, each group should list two to five questions that ONLY that person can answer.] Do not ask them questions that could easily be found on the internet. Some examples of questions might include:

- What made you become interested in _____?
- How long have you been working with _____?
- What solutions do you see as having the most potential?
- What advice do you have for anyone who is interested in solving ___?
- Are there other organizations that you'd suggest us contacting that might be interested in partnering with us?
- What do you believe to be the biggest problem with this issue?

Thank you so very much for your time. We look forward to hearing from you as you help further our goals to address this issue.

Sincerely,

First name, Last name
First name, Last name
Contact information (email/phone number)

Conducting Interviews—When conducting interviews, it is important that the interviewee feel safe and comfortable (Rubin and Rubin 2012). Students can do this by thinking of the interview as a conversation as opposed to a strict series of questions that must be adhered to at all costs.

It may be important to be able to compare answers to similar questions between different stakeholders, so it will be important to ask the same questions of multiple people, even though they might come at a different point in each interview. If students are trying to identify the causes of the issue, the lived experiences for those dealing with the issue, and the solutions to the issue, their questions should include what the individuals think around these ideas.

Equally important, when they are conducting their interviews, students must keep themselves safe. While there is certainly valuable information to be found regarding homelessness from people who are homeless, for example, students should not take it upon themselves to approach individuals on their own. A shelter worker may be able to identify safe interview subjects, provide a safe location for interviews, or accompany the student as part of an interview team, as well as answering questions based on their own knowledge and experience.

Capturing Interview Information—In order for the students to capture everything that is being said, while also allowing for the conversational approach to occur, they should plan to audio-record the interviews so they can be fully present in the conversation. Most smartphones have a voice memo feature, and the microphones typically do a decent job of capturing audio recordings. Once the student has an audio file, they might want to create a printed transcript of the audio file to refer back to more easily. It is important that the interviewee is aware and gives permission to be recorded.

Presentation Activities

As Jerry Seinfeld (1999) once quipped, people who have to go to a funeral would rather be dead than be the ones giving the eulogy as the fear of public speaking supersedes the fear of death. However, state standards typically include speaking and listening as an aspect of required skills. Having students present their research findings to the class in a structured way allows students to be exposed to the very necessary skill of speaking in front of the classroom. Students might include the following information in their presentations:

- Definition of the Issue: They should explain what the issue is, where it occurs, and who is affected by the issue. For example, if students have chosen poverty, they might want to explain what the official poverty line is, and how that can differ from community to community.
- Causes and Effects of the Issue: They should do the best they can to clarify what the causes and effects are of their issue utilizing the information they discovered from their article annotation, as well as from their problem tree. If they can support this part of their presentation with research, they should be encouraged to include citations. This might also be an opportunity for students to include primary research. If they interviewed someone, they might incorporate a quote in their presentation in order to humanize the issue, and help to show the relevance.
- Stakeholders: They should include who the people are that are involved with the issue from all levels. Who are the people who suffer from the issue? Who are the people who benefit from the issue? Who are the people who are trying to do work to solve the issue?
- Solutions So Far: They might also include solutions that have been attempted up to this point. Obviously, they will be developing their own solutions, but it would be good for them to discuss the ideas that have been attempted, particularly if they want to think about their own solution in more significant ways.

Table 3.3 at the end of this chapter provides links to resources on preparing effective presentations and a general rubric for evaluating presentations.

PUTTING THEORY INTO PRACTICE

Each teacher will apply this curriculum slightly differently to suit their students and standards. For example, while high school teachers may focus on having students read contemporary news pieces in order to address the nonfiction requirements of the common core, junior high teachers may encourage students to focus more on interviewing their peers and teachers in the school, depending upon the school culture.

Teachers at all levels who have followed this curriculum identified one common factor, however, that was critical for success. All of them spent a significant amount of time conferencing with students as they developed their approach to the final action plan. It was these one-on-one conferences that truly helped both the teacher and the students identify opportunities for solutions. Through the iterative conversations that occurred, all parties involved were able to be creative in their final approach.

Successes

While the curriculum effectively helps students develop skills in research, writing, and presentation, some of its most meaningful successes come from empowering students to engage with important issues in their communities.

A Response from the Mayor—The emails can be quite powerful due to their ability to connect an "expert" in the field who might participate in the students' growth as an activist. One example, detailed below, came from a senior student who had previously told the teacher that setting a limo up for her homecoming was more important than paying attention in class.

Prior to the federal passage of same-sex marriage, this student was focused on LGBTQ rights in Arizona, where politicians tend to lean toward the conservative side and are reluctant to prioritize LGBTQ rights. She had emailed multiple politicians and leaders in the community with no response. On the way into school one day, the teacher heard a piece about how the mayor of a small town in Southern Arizona had legalized same-sex marriage for a day before the attorney general threatened to prosecute her. The teacher encouraged her student to reach out to that mayor.

The following day, she came flying into the room more excited than she had been all semester. She was on cloud nine about the fact that the mayor had immediately responded to her and spoke with her as an adult about what she might do to address the discrimination against same-sex marriage in

Arizona. The student actually thought her mother was posing as the mayor since she had been so discouraged prior to that email.

After that moment, she was absolutely engaged in the rest of the project. Although they did not hear back from the majority of "experts" she contacted, when she finally did, it was incredible. It was this respect from an adult that allowed this to happen.

Finding an Ally in the School Principal—Additional successes happened when the students reached out to the adults on their campus. The junior high students went to their principal and were able to discuss assembly topics with her that they felt passionate about. They left feeling as though they had a say in the school's operations and an ally in their action plan.

Finding a Voice—Another high school set of students interviewed the English as a Second Language (ESL) teacher on campus and were able to identify a more concrete approach to their action plan through that interaction. This also empowered them to feel comfortable reaching out to other powerful adults in the school community beyond their campus.

Generating Empathy and Engagement—The presentations were also quite successful for those who opted to do an informational presentation prior to the final product. Many students stated that they wished they could group up with other students in the class or learn more about the issue because they were interested in what others were doing. This generative empathy creation can be powerful on its own and bodes well for continued civic engagement by the students.

Struggles

Lest you believe that this is all sunshine and roses, there are difficulties in this area of the work. Two aspects of this phase seem to present difficulties more often than others.

Lack of Response from Stakeholders and Allies—Asking students to email strangers is not necessarily difficult to do to begin with; however, getting a response back can be far more difficult. It is important to not tie a response to any sort of grade or evaluative measure. Sometimes the students are unable to articulate their ideas in writing, and as multiple groups are emailing multiple stakeholders, you may not be able to help them shape their emails as well as you'd like.

Upon conferencing with several of the groups who complained about not hearing back from anyone, it was easy to understand why after reading their emails. While the messages may have been formatted properly based on the template, the content did not clearly articulate the purpose of the email. If you ensure that the students have developed questions with a strong purpose, this may alleviate this concern. Additionally, it might be good to try to get other eyes on the email and the subsequent questions through peer review prior to sending them.

Fitting Activities into Time Available—Another difficulty is the time frame. In order to fully understand the complexities of these big issues students tend to pick, there needs to be a great deal of research conducted, and knowledge gained. Picking the primary issue to address may seem easy upon an initial glance, but as students learn more, they often realize that they are not as well prepared as they had previously thought.

Flexibility and the ability for students to continually revise their thinking in this area will be critical, although, at some point, they will have to make a final decision and stick with it if they are going to be able to finish. Providing students with timelines to work through certain steps will help, in addition to being flexible with your own evaluative process.

CONCLUSION

This section of the project is the one that looks the most significantly different from teacher to teacher. The one constant with everyone has been a sense of independent learning from the students. This is the time when the students are making the most connections, having the most discussion, and driving their own learning. Whichever direction you end up taking your students, remember the primary goal of this section is for students to obtain knowledge outside of the novel from both primary and secondary research, identify what specifically they want to know about their issue, and find ways to begin presenting what they know to others. Hopefully, these activities will provide support for you as you move forward with this activity.

Chapter 4

Taking Action

Typically, people don't think of tenth graders as being the voice of persuasion with members of the school board, but with the right encouragement and opportunity, they can become exactly that. Four sophomores in an honors English class opted to address the systemic inequities of instructional design by writing a letter about English-only mandates to their school board. Most students would feel powerless in the face of the official school curriculum.

These four students, however, personally related to their book's protagonist, who, like them, was unable to speak English on the first day of school. They also saw the struggles of their newly immigrated peers firsthand in their core classes.

One of the students, Luisa, for example, translated nearly all of a peer's biology materials for her, but the English language learner was still failing the course because Luisa couldn't help her on tests. This inspired Luisa's group to send the school board a letter requesting that more accommodations be made in order to help students like this, who were capable of doing the work but unable to access the material or demonstrate their knowledge due to a language barrier.

While state laws prohibited the district school board from making such changes to the curriculum, the student group received an immediate response from the board requesting a meeting among the group, the principal, and themselves to come up with ideas that might be within the scope of the laws that could still provide the necessary support these emerging bilingual students needed.

The idea that students could generate the desire for a meeting between themselves and the board members of the largest school district in the state is powerful. Although the students themselves could not fix the issue on their own, they were able to leverage their skills to move forward in addressing

Table 4.1 Activity Overview

Teacher Does	Students Do
Develop students' agency	Develop action plan
Provide ideas	Implement action plan
Check in with and guide groups	Present the results of their plan

the issue in very real ways. This is the type of work that can come out of this curriculum.

This chapter provides insight into the ways students can follow up on the research and knowledge gained from reading. While this section is the most difficult to explain in a linear fashion, it is arguably the most important aspect to the project for the students. Not all students will have the same results, but the idea that they are able to take action is a powerful one and allows multiple ways for students to become productive citizens in their world (table 4.1).

WHAT THE TEACHER DOES

In order to prepare students to take action within their community, the teacher must support students in ways that give them a sense of power. The teacher plays three important roles at this stage: a coach, encouraging students' agency; an idea bank, helping students find ways to achieve their goals; and a liaison between the students and others. Be prepared to have a sense of controlled chaos in the classroom! Students will be working individually or in small groups, and the teacher will need to consistently check in with all of them to understand what each group or individual needs to move forward

Student Agency

Merriam-Webster defines agency as "the capacity, condition, or state of acting or exerting power." Students must have a sense of autonomy regarding the direction their plan takes, and they also must feel that what they do can make an impact.

To achieve this goal, teachers give students free rein to design their own action plans, to the extent possible. While the actions students can take are limited by time and funding, the teacher should not provide so much guidance to students that it reduces their sense of agency. Some students will certainly ask for more guidance and structure, but many will feel honored that they have an opportunity to create something that has the potential to make the world a better place.

Taking Action 51

In order for students to feel as though their project or work might have some sort of impact on the world at large, there ought to be a concrete way for students to take their ideas out of your classroom. Developing an action plan or taking action affords an excellent opportunity for an authentic performance task, as well, which supports the idea that what we are doing in the classroom matters.

Idea Bank

It is important that students see you as a resource for ideas. While students should ultimately make their own decisions and feel they can spread their wings with this project, they will very often feel unsure of where to start. This is where you can help them come up with concepts that might be fitting for both school settings and more expansive community-based projects.

Examples of ideas students have completed or conceptualized for this project include the following. Some of these are described in more detail at the end of this chapter in the "successes" section.

- A full color, glossy page, bound magazine that explores specific issues (e.g., LGBTQ experiences, or a collection of immigration resources)
- Collection boxes for donations (e.g., school supplies for students in need, or money to sponsor refugee families)
- Phone applications that support students experiencing personal trauma (e.g., a bullying hotline, or emotional support student center)
- Videos, posters and brochures to be circulated through the school and community (e.g., interviews with students about their experiences with racism, or brochures that include resources for students dealing with poverty)
- Outreach programs that focus on a variety of issues from special needs students to quality of life issues (e.g., school clubs like Amnesty International or Gay, Lesbian and Straight Supporters [GLASS])
- Social media accounts to raise awareness (e.g., Instagram accounts to spread information about climate change)

Take care to provide multiple examples. If you only suggest one idea, it may limit the students' conceptualization about the directions their own project might take. In the very first iteration of this project, the teacher only showed students a brochure to illustrate what they might do. Perhaps unsurprisingly, 90 percent of the students submitted a brochure as their plan of action.

Some students' action plan ideas may be too big to complete during the time allowed, and both student and teacher will need to think creatively about how to use those ideas. For example, one young woman proposed to write a book about poverty to raise awareness, as her own reading of a YA novel had done for her. She previously hadn't thought she could ever have anything in common with someone in poverty, and it was a book that made her "see them as people." In this case, the teacher asked the student to generate a long-term plan with the idea that she might enact a first step toward the long-term goal.

School-Communication

Make sure your school administrators are looped into your ultimate curriculum goals for this project. Students may be creating posters that they want to put up around the school, asking to present to other classrooms, or requesting meetings with school officials. Administrators who understand the purpose of the curriculum can provide important support. Additionally, if a community member reaches out to the administrator based upon contact from your students, the administrator should be forearmed with the knowledge about what you are attempting to do.

You can also support your students' activities by identifying teachers who are receptive to students presenting in their classrooms and connecting students with administrators who might be able to support or mayimpede students as they implement their action plans. Unfortunately, some adults—even adults who work in schools—do not trust that students are capable of making change and may not be receptive to students taking action outside of the classroom. This is where you can help be a buffer between those naysayers and your students.

Conferencing with Student Groups

Developing a plan to act is the most significant aspect of this section of the curriculum and can be the most daunting. In order to ensure that students are working on their projects, you will need to meet with them often. It is a good idea to keep a log sheet of each group where you can list their ideas, the date that you checked in with them, and what actions you might take to support their work. It might look like the information found in table 4.2.

As you can see from the chart, the students' ideas changed over time. Their action items will also change. There may be some things that the students want to do in the beginning, although over time they may realize their resources of time or energy are limited, and as such, they may end up needing to shift their idea. You should encourage some ebb and flow of ideas, even if it feels unsettling for you and the students, although you may need to help them land somewhere eventually.

If you keep a log of this information, you can help guide them to still stay true to their purpose, while also supporting them to bite off smaller chunks,

Table 4.2   Conference Check-in Example

Topic _____ Book _____
Group Members_____

Date	Ideas	Actionable Items
3/5	Write a new law about X	Find local politician's names, Research existing laws, research policy around X
3/7	Email the senator about X so they can write a new law	Find contact info for senator
3/9	Begin an information campaign	Research most effective ways of communicating
3/11	Continue information campaign	Continue work on developing platform Talk to administration about sharing platform (teacher or student)

as opposed to trying to go too big, failing, and giving up. (It is very important to help them feel some modicum of success!) Even sending an email to a senator or congressperson can be very rewarding, even if nothing ultimately comes of it.

Teachers know that big changes tend to move slowly, so it is critical to make sure that students feel some sense of efficacy (Pajares 2003) in order to continue their work. As educators, our primary goal is to create transfer of knowledge, and one way to do this is by ensuring that students feel they can continue to make change in the world in some way, shape, or form.

THINKING THROUGH IT

For the teacher, the action phase of the project can be the most rewarding and the most frustrating part of the curriculum. It may feel as though your students are not making progress, although it will be a positive move if you can be okay with living in the chaos. As long as students are continuing to communicate with one another and are intentionally working toward making change, you will see success.

Barriers Students Might Have around the Issues Themselves

Some students will choose difficult topics because they are immersed in them. Sometimes these strong feelings can become barriers to developing an action plan. For example, some students choose to focus on mental illness as their topic, sometimes because they have struggled with eating disorders or depression themselves. Students who are being bullied may choose bullying as a topic. These are often the same students who feel helpless to solve the issue.

If a student seems to have no idea regarding how to begin an action plan or seems stuck with making decisions about how to address the issue, this may be a flag indicating the student is dealing with a serious problem and needs help. Bringing in counselors or school psychologists may be appropriate. The teacher can gently couple this with actions to help these students develop some sense of agency and control around their own issues.

One such student talked about developing an anonymous app where students could use it as an open journaling opportunity and "workers" would respond with kind and supportive thoughts to the person who is struggling. While the app itself did not actually get created in the time frame that was afforded, the idea behind it might allow the student to think through other ways to make it happen in the future.

Troubleshooting and Supplying Innovative Approaches

Many of your students will begin this project with an idealistic view, which is wonderful! Allow your students to take this "change the world" approach to begin with, and count on their enthusiasm to boost their creativity and learning. This idealism, however, can lead to a sense of failure very rapidly.

If students are focused on a major issue that has gone unsolved for years, it can feel quite daunting to figure out where to begin. Spreading awareness is certainly always an option, and can be powerful, but if students feel as though their work is just another classroom assignment, it may not have the desired effect on the transfer of knowledge we are hoping for. This is where you, as the expert facilitator, can come into play.

Pointing students toward podcasts or people in the world doing the work they want to be doing can be inspirational. One teacher listened to National Public Radio (NPR) on her way into school every day and said it felt as though every day she heard a new story that was connected to the students' topics in some way. The teacher could then support the students by sharing a name or an interview that they could follow up on. This often led them to consider different ways to tackle the problem.

One of her students was focused on LGBTQ rights, for example, and the teacher heard a story about a mayor of a small town in the same state who had legalized gay marriage. The order only lasted a day before the state's attorney general threatened to sue the town. The teacher gave the student the mayor's name, and the mayor responded to the student's email immediately, suggesting different ways the student might take action. By knowing the student's topic, and keeping her ears open to the world around her, the teacher was able to help the student make a significant connection.

Students' own experiences can also be a source of knowledge or ideas. The group that wrote the letter to the school board about English-only practices originally chose immigration as their issue. Immigration is an enormous topic that befuddles many people. The students needed to find a bite-sized piece they could tackle.

The teacher conferenced with those students and asked them what they most identified with in the book. Together, they discovered that most of them had struggled with learning English upon their own immigration to the United States, although those students had immigrated in friendlier times for English language learners. These students no longer needed bilingual education, but they recognized the added difficulties more recent immigrants faced. It was this experience that led them to an innovative approach to dealing with an issue related to immigration.

STUDENT ACTIVITIES

At this stage of the project, student activities focus on developing an action plan, implementing it, and presenting the results of their work. This portion of the curriculum addresses a wide variety of Common Core State Standards through authentic performance tasks. This section explains how student plans might be developed and suggests ways to assess student contribution for each section.

Develop the Work Plan

A quick Google search for action plans will yield multiple results, although several are not necessarily appropriate for the purposes of this project. All the plans do have several commonalities, including

- a list of goals,
- a list of tasks and who from the group will do them, and
- deadlines for accomplishing the tasks.

Some templates begin with a long-term goal and then break that down into more achievable short-term goals. This might allow your students to begin with their lofty, idealistic goal, but then ultimately focus on just completing a more manageable goal during your class time.

What is important about the work plan is that the guide breaks the project down into tasks and provides group members accountability to ensure more equitable contributions throughout the process. Table 4.3 is one example of an accountability worksheet you might use.

A more detailed guide that might give you more information about the process the students went through, as well as giving students guidance about what they ought to be thinking about can be found in table 4.4.

Table 4.3 Action Plan Work Plan

Project Name

Team Members

Product/Plan/Outcomes   Due

What needs to be done?   Who will do this part?   By when?   X=Done

---

Present Results to Stakeholders in the Community

A critical aspect of engaging in a civic manner is reaching out to community members. This step requires students to follow up on their previous research about who in the community is already doing this work, and who might be available to help in terms of taking action.

At this stage of the curriculum, it is important that students are thoughtful about what they want from these stakeholders. Do they want them to take specific steps to serve the ultimate action plan, or is their goal to provide information that will influence the stakeholders' future decisions regarding the issue?

Table 4.4 Action Plan Template

Summary	This section will summarize the problem in one or two sentences, and give a brief overview of the planned solution.
Introduction	This section will give the research behind the issue, including the causes and effects that the students have identified. This will also include any previously done research about prior action that has been taken.
Needs/Problems	This section will specifically identify the needs that the students and community have identified as important to address. This may differ from research, depending upon the students' specific needs.
Goals/Objectives	This section will include the students' goals for addressing the project. This will allow students to clearly lay out what they hope to address, with the understanding that directly eliminating the issue is rarely an option. This may include several levels of goals that range from highly idealistic, to short-term beginning goals.
Procedures	This should lay out the specific procedures that the students will follow in order to take action.
Timetable	This should lay out the specific dates of each step the students might take in order to enact change. This allows students to see how action might occur in various stages, and allow them to remain encouraged even if the semester doesn't allow for them to complete the project.
Budget	This section will include a potential budget for the project, which may encourage students to think more broadly, and more hypothetically, which might help spur them to take definitive steps that might lead up to action.
Stakeholders/ Personnel	This section could include the people who would be impacted by and would impact the change. Who all needs to be involved to make this work successfully?
Evaluation	This section might include the steps that the team would take to decide whether to not the program was working. This may explore the way the project could be implemented, or it might include continuing research that shows that change is happening.
Next Steps	The final section may include steps that should be taken after the plan is initiated. This could take many forms depending upon how far into the project your students are able to get.

Contacts that might be accessible to students include the following:

- The local or state school board or individual board members
- The city council or its members, and other local officials
- Nonprofit and civic organizations (e.g., United Way)
- State legislators, and other state officials and administrators
- Members of the U.S. Congress and Senate representing the students' district

Students may invite stakeholders into the classroom or ask to go out and speak to stakeholders and present their work to them.

This step in the project provides a wonderful opportunity for students to learn how to make contact with individuals in their local society that have power, and ideally, recognize that they may have a voice in the way their community views or deals with this issue.

Reach Out to School Administrators

Similar to community stakeholders, school administrators can be very powerful forces in supporting a student's action plan. Many school administrators are former teachers who miss the positive student interaction they had when they spent time in their own classrooms. The project can provide an opportunity to bridge the gap between the classroom and the administration in powerful ways. Students can influence school policy or, conversely, gain a better understanding of the factors that constrain what administrators can do. This may have a hidden benefit of helping students be more creative in the way they approach problem-solving at the school level, if they are disavowed of the notion that adults in higher positions can "fix" everything.

As students are not typically in positions to be initiating meetings, they may need to be taught how to make appointments and how to navigate the potential need to work through a busy administrator's assistant. It may be a good idea to have the student(s) conduct a mock meeting with you prior to meeting with the administrator so you can avoid any potential confusion between the goals of the project and the student(s)' message.

Present to the School

The work students are doing is important. As such, other students need to know about the issue and these projects. Since students have probably been focused on this work for a while, and they are now sharing what they intend to do about it, you will often find that they do not struggle from a lack of talking points.

In your own classroom, you might have them present their final action plans to their peers as a spoken word presentation. A Pecha Kucha, described in textbox 4.1, is a great way to do this. The Pecha Kucha provides a highly structured format that requires students to keep their focus and limits how long they can speak. This avoids what happened in an early iteration of this project, when one student spoke for almost an entire class period about his project. While it was important and compelling, the class schedule does not typically allow for such long presentations.

TEXTBOX 4.1

The Pecha Kucha, which means chit chat, is a 400 second (6.6 minute) presentation that consists of twenty slides that are on a timer set to switch every 20 seconds. The idea is that the presenter will use pictures to emphasize his or her points so they are not reading off the slides, helping them to be more engaging. This also keeps the presentation times very structured without you having to be the timekeeper. You can find more information at pechakucha.com.

Students can also present their work to their peers outside of their own classroom. Ways to achieve this include the following:

- Individual classroom presentations, in person or through a prepared video
- Public Service Announcement (PSAs) that are created and played through the school's video production class, if available
- Presenting action plans science fair style: each student group has a table and finds a way to present their projects, while community members and parents visit the tables to hear what the students have developed. This is also a fantastic way to generate community support for the students' projects and your school.

Assessments

Assessment of this stage can be tricky, as what students plan to do, and what they end up doing may differ for a variety of reasons. As such, it is important to avoid evaluating the students on their finished results, as it may limit their idea potential, or cause you to have to give students grades that you may not feel they fully deserve.

If you were to take a collaborative approach to the project, you might give the groups credit for evenly distributing a workload that seems doable, yet also ambitious. If you were to take a more goal-oriented approach, it might make more sense to focus on their ability to take a task and break it down into manageable and logical steps that clearly delineate what the students might do in their work. While you want to give the students feedback, and most likely will need to assign some form of credit to the students for this work, this is a difficult place for a rubric to be utilized due to the iterative nature of the work. If, however, you and your students want a rubric, table 4.5 might be a good start.

Table 4.5 Final Rubric

Final Action Plan Rubric
Student Name(s) _____
Class _____ Date _____
Chosen issue _____

	Rating=4	Rating=3	Rating=2	Rating=1	Score
Defining the problem	Student(s) state the problem clearly and identify underlying issues	Student(s) define the problem adequately, although may be limited in examples	Student(s) fail to define the problem adequately, causing confusion	Student(s) fail to identify the core problem of focus	
Developing a plan to address the issue	Student(s) develop a clear and concise plan to solve the problem, and have begun to enact the plan	Student(s) develop an adequate plan although they do not take steps to enact the plan	Student(s) develop a marginal plan, and do not follow it to its conclusion	Student(s) do not develop a coherent plan to address the issue	
Collecting and Analyzing information	Student(s) collect information from multiple sources and use it to develop their plan	Student(s) collect adequate information and incorporate some of it into their plan	Student(s) collect inadequate information to be fully useful for their plan	Student(s) collected no viable information	
Communication	Student(s) clearly present their work to others in ways that are inspiring	Student(s) clearly present their work to others	Student(s) are somewhat unclear in their sharing of information to others	Student(s) did not share their information with others.	

Total score

PUTTING THEORY INTO PRACTICE

Successes

Throughout this curriculum, most students are self-motivated and engaged because the project is ultimately theirs from the beginning to the end. While the final products may not always be as lofty as the students' initial iterations, there are a great many successes to be had.

Some of the successes include the following:

- Magazine—A group developed a magazine that focused on the transition of a school wrestler from female to male over the course of four years. The subject of the magazine provided pictures from her junior high years, and then ultimately his high school years after his transformation. The group interviewed the young man, and he was able to explain his process, fears, and rationale in a full and detailed way. The magazine was printed on glossy paper and distributed (with permission) to members of the school.
- Collection boxes—Several student groups created collection boxes and placed them around their schools to gather school supplies and various items that others around the campus or in the community might need.
- Documentary film—One set of students interviewed students about times they had experienced racism, put the interviews together into a documentary-style film, and then showed the film to other classrooms on campus and had an open discussion about racism in their community.
- Social media—One set of students created an Instagram page that posts facts and images about the environment, in addition to interviews with individuals on their campus about what they might know or not know.
- School assembly—A young woman spoke to her principal about hosting a school-wide assembly that would explain the dangers of human trafficking and wanted to begin working on developing a safe space for students to stay at school until their parents came home from work.
- Clubs—Several groups of students have started clubs at their schools including GLASS and Amnesty International.
- Letters—Students have written letters to their local authority figures from the school board, to the local politicians to focus on specific issues that have a more local impact.

Struggles

In asking students to create and carry out an action plan, roadblocks can arise.

The first, and most pressing, is the reality of having limited time. Students will often struggle to identify a specific focus in the beginning, and by the time they have come up with a solid action plan, you may be out of time. Additionally, the varying nature of the student groups and their plans means that the students will often be on different timelines, and while one group may still be struggling to get started, another group may almost be done with their plan.

It is probably better to err on the side of caution and give students slightly less time than some of them want. This will avoid losing educational time for students who are taking a less involved approach to the plan.

Another potential struggle is resistance to the project. This may come from students, administrators, or the community. The solution depends on the nature of the resistance:

- Provide Choice—If you do not provide your students with as much choice as possible, they may feel you are pushing an agenda. Acknowledge their interests and allow them to approach the issue in their own ways. Be prepared for students to see the issue differently than you do after reading the novel and working through the curriculum.
- Find Alternative Ways to Success—After reading the novel and working through the curriculum, some students may believe that no action is necessary. Perhaps asking students to take on more of an analytic approach to the issue may be helpful. Their presentation could take the form of exploring the value of what is already being done around the issue. Their plan might be focused around developing a way to research the effectiveness of whatever is currently done. Again this goes back to the choice. Students may not want to participate in something that moves beyond the traditional trope of a classroom, which is often teacher-centered evaluation. While this is unfortunate and unlikely, it may be a reality, and you should not take it personally.
- Keep Administrators Informed—Make sure administrators understand the learning goals behind the curriculum, and the ways that students are demonstrating mastery of CCSS through their research, public outreach, writing, and speaking. This can mitigate resistance from administrators at school systems already under public fire for inequitable practices, for example, who may see students as adding fuel to the fire. Sometimes administrators just get frustrated by the number of posters put up in hallways and want to see a cleaner looking campus.
- Coach Students on Effective Communication—The school community may push back if they perceive students as overstepping their boundaries while pursuing action. It may also be useful to discuss tact with your students. Refer students back to Adichie's "Danger of a Single Story" and warn them about having a single story about the issues they are tackling. All that being said, they may experience resistance simply because people often prefer to

keep the status quo, but effective communication may bring them closer to their goals than confrontational speaking styles.

CONCLUSION

The action phase of the curriculum can be the most rewarding part of the project for you and your students. Seeing them carry out plans that they developed and feel passionate about, regardless of their success, is powerful and heart-warming. As an educator, this will be the part of the school year that will be the most energizing. These benefits will only occur if you remain flexible. For students to do their best work on this project, they must have ownership of their work, and you are there to act as a facilitator, cheerleader, and guide.

Enjoy the fruits of your students' labor at the end of this work, and recognize that you have made significant strides toward making the world a better place.

Chapter 5

Voices from the Field

While I primarily pulled the material for this text from the teachers' and students' reflections, I wanted to share their own voices without my meddling. The following interviews with a seventh grade teacher who just wrapped up his third year of teaching, a tenth grade teacher who just wrapped up her sixth year of teaching and a seventh grade student who went through the curriculum this year show insight about the aspects of the project that impacted them in significant ways as well as their takeaways.

I encourage you to consider the different ways each of these individuals experienced the curriculum, and ponder how your own prior knowledge and context might impact your own experience. Each of these individuals speaks to the power of this work, even though they are all in vastly different spaces, and I hope that you find their words as inspiring as I do.

TEACHER 1: MR. MUÑOZ

Mr. Muñoz was a third-year teacher, at the time of this interview, who was still considered probationary by California credentialing standards. He is constantly self-reflective, and somewhat hyper-critical of his own teaching. He cares deeply and passionately about his students and their successes, and is willing to do whatever it takes to help them achieve success in their coursework. In this interview, he expresses his newfound admiration for his students, his willingness to support his students through pushback, what he felt like his students learned, how he measured it, what realizations he had around the psychological impact of books, and the importance of this work for long-term change.

Dr. Hays: So, I really want the readers to have a chance to hear directly from teachers who've done this curriculum. My first question for you is: Do you feel like you see your students differently in any way?

Mr. Muñoz: In having to ask them the question of what do they believe is wrong with society, and what do they believe that can be fixed, I was really taken aback by how quick they were to bring up issues that they think are important. And a lot of those issues were, of course, obviously relevant to them. Also, it was very surprising considering how much thought they put into it, and how much of the responsibility they took on how much they showed that they cared. That was very surprising as well. It was very exciting to see my students put so much thought into their projects.

Dr. Hays: Right. Yeah, I love that. You talked about some of it being relevant, obviously it was all relevant to them, but what were some of the surprising topics that they picked that you maybe were not expecting?

Mr. Muñoz: A lot of them said, "recycling," which was one. Another one was human trafficking. For recycling, it was awesome, because they were thinking about how wasteful the school is, how much paper we waste, plastic, Styrofoam, all sorts of materials that the school uses . . . and then they went to the school to figure out what they can do to implement some recycling processes. They became very surprised when they learned that the school has nothing in place for actual recycling. And they were sort of taken aback by that and at that point they took it upon themselves to implement some sort of system so that we can recycle. And I've actually taken that to heart, because now I have a box in my classroom dedicated to paper. I don't like wasting paper. Anytime I have the opportunity to recycle paper, I do it. And that was sort of inspired by them.

Another instance was for human trafficking last year. I had a group of pretty high-level students who were very grade oriented. So, their dedication to the project wasn't that surprising, but how I saw them go about it was amazing. They came up with an idea for a coin drive and they came up with their own speech to go to every classroom and politely ask to help out with their cause. And by the end of the project, they had raised close to 200 dollars, which is really cool. And they were super excited to know that they contributed something to combat or to fight against human trafficking. They were very pleased with themselves, and I was very pleased to see that too.

Dr. Hays: That's so awesome. I love that.

Mr. Muñoz: Yeah. I mean when they were reading *Sold* [by Patricia McCormick] for human trafficking, they were just completely flabbergasted by all of the things that happened in the text and they were just like, "Wow, this type of thing really happened? Like this is a true story?" And they were just like, "Oh man." And I really felt that that drove them to do something tangible, that they could contribute for the cause. And so, I really feel like that fueled their need to help.

Dr. Hays: Okay, so now in this project . . . you've done it twice now. I'm sure that things have come up in terms of organization or student reactions, parent reactions, and administration reactions. What are some things that you would recommend to people getting ready to begin this project?

Mr. Muñoz: Number one, know the process and if you're implementing this process with multiple teachers, make sure everyone's on the same page the entire way. Because with Mr. Frost and Flores, with the lit circles, we all did like lit circles a little differently each time. Just make sure that they know what to do and when. A second recommendation I have would be to ensure that all of the major players in your school are aware of what you're doing before you get into the thick of it, because then you won't have to worry as much as to how the administration will react. Before I even started the project the first year, I went to Swearinger [the principal] and I told her that "I plan on doing this project and these students are going to intend to do something in their school and it's going to be everywhere and just be prepared for that."

And she was all for it. One little pushback I got though for the first year and the second year was that she didn't want to put any emphasis on LGBTQ issues, which I was kind of disappointed about, because I had a student that was actually considered trans, and she identified as a male, or he identified as a male, and I really wanted to support him and let him know that I approve of what he wanted to do. But the school just wasn't ready for it. The town that I work in is considered to be ten years behind. Might even be more. They're still in the 1990s if anything. So it might be even useful to, if you have that sort of push back at your site, to decide [ahead of time] how you want to deal with these issues. If a kid wants to do LGBTQ stuff, maybe you could do it from a different avenue, but still hit that issue. Just so that kids, when they have an idea to pursue something, aren't immediately shut down. They can pursue what they believe is right.

Dr. Hays: So maybe like identity might be another way to frame it instead of LGBTQ issues.

Mr. Muñoz: For sure. Or just maybe tolerance. That'd be a great way to put it. Having kids pursue tolerance in every aspect possible no matter what. These last two years, I haven't had any of those students who are obviously LGBTQ. It would be great to see again, so I could try to do it differently. Because I'm pretty sure the first time I had to pull him aside and was like, "I love you as my student and you're a great kid and I love that you want to pursue this kind of idea, but the school just isn't ready for it yet. And I'm sorry." And if I could change how I went about it, I totally would. I would just say, "Do this. Follow your dreams. Show the world what's right." And if it comes up again, I'm definitely going to do it that way. If I get pushback, then I'll just say, "I'm more of an accepting person of modern ideas and I'm not trying to hold these students back." Yeah. I would be willing to defend my students for it.

Dr. Hays: That's powerful. So what was the most surprising thing that you experienced?

Mr. Muñoz: Besides the LGBTQ pushback, toward the end of the project when I was having kids gather evidence of what they have accomplished it feels good to see that they were really proud of what they accomplished. They thought of something, they did it, and they saw some effect from it. They know they accomplished something and then they know in the future they can do it again. That was the greatest thing for me, being able to see kids promote actual progress in their school.

Dr. Hays: Right. So, okay, which kind of makes me think, as you're talking, I'm thinking there's so many amazing things about this project. Do you think it would have been worth it if you had to get your own books instead of having them provided for you?

Mr. Muñoz: Yes. Yeah, I think it would have been worth it. Yeah. The original text we taught is kind of dry. And even [the teachers] said it was dry and the fact that we were able to provide new interesting texts, and the students all got to choose their own, so they felt like it was for them was way more important, because a lot of the times, these kids, they're in a low-income area, a lot of times they feel like they get the bottom of the bucket. Or if not that, they just get the same thing everyone else gets, and it's like they don't feel like an individual who can express themselves in their own way. And when you give them the opportunity to come up with their own ideas, they really take it. It's very organic. And I love brainstorming with them. They come up to me and say, "Well Mr. Muñoz, what do you think about this?"

Last year I had some kids, and they were stuck. They were focused on bullying, and one group was just like, "I don't know what to do. I want to spread the message to not bully, but I don't know how to do it." And so I went through all my own literature and I found examples of zines that I've had from kids, people my age, and other sources, and I showed them how awesome it is to make your own booklet. As soon as I showed them how to do it, they went for it. With a little guidance, they put out a really awesome project. It was a cool zine and people were super impressed by it. And they felt so cool to have their own little book.

They're in eighth grade now and whenever they see me, they're like, "Hey Mr. Muñoz." That exact same group, they always say "What's up?" to me. They're always happy to see me and the effect of that might not be apparent now, but eventually they will remember back in seventh grade where they made something and they will know that they can do it again.

Dr. Hays: That's awesome, which brings me to another question. So, you had them in seventh grade, and now they're in eighth grade on campus. Do you see any residual effects on those eighth graders?

Mr. Muñoz: One student in particular, his name's Elton. My boy, Elton. I can just tell he holds his head higher. I really do think that the fact that I let so much responsibility go to them, they really took it to heart and they felt more mature because of it. And they felt they can hold their head up a little higher. I had this student last year and I really don't think he was that confident all year. He seemed as though he was on the fringe. He didn't feel like he was generally accepted.

I spoke to him throughout the year like, "Yo, man. You are who you are, and you have to accept it and as soon as you do, people will love you for it." And then implementing this project where he focused on bullying, and putting out this zine, seriously raised his confidence. It made him aware that he was able to be mature and responsible and that he is capable and he is a cool kid. Just because he might look a little different does not make him any worse or any better than anyone else. And I really do think he accepted himself more because of it.

I had another student, who struggled academically the entire year. He could not write. He could not read that well, but when it came to spreading his message of bullying he made these badges and he went around having people recite a pledge [to not bully others]. He was proud to do it, and it raised his confidence so he was more able to express himself to other people without having to feel like he was being judged.

Dr. Hays: That's awesome. Okay, so now what were the most difficult things?

Mr. Muñoz: So for me, the first two years of teaching, I was super hands-on. I'm super neurotic and I really wanted my kids to do well. I was very insecure about my teaching and whether or not the students were able to grasp what I was talking about. This curriculum really made me let them go without having to helicopter over them and make sure they're doing what they need to be doing.

One big struggle for me was time, trying to figure out how kids can make it through the book on time by the end of the project to sort of get the full force of the book. Many of them did not finish reading in the time given, and we had to go on to the research project, but I figured at least they were exposed to the idea.

But a lot of the time when they were working during the research portion, and they felt like they had finished, I noticed they often said, "Mr. Muñoz, can I read that text now? Can I read that book that I missed out on?" It's like, "Yes, go finish it. Go finish it." Some of the kids finished it, and that made me feel really good. Because they cared about what was going on in the book. They cared about their issue. And that sort of drove them to continue to make sure they're doing what they need to be doing.

Dr. Hays: So understanding that much of this work is independent, how do you know that they are doing what they need to be doing?

Mr. Muñoz: I told them, "If you guys want to show me evidence, I need to see pictures. I need to see receipts, I need to see emails, I need to see something to show me you made an effort." The most prevalent evidence was definitely photos. That was the easiest way to show that they had accomplished stuff. They would go around taking pictures of the poster they put up or them working together or the people they've tried to contact, the money they raised, the badges that they've passed out, and the zines that I saw people reading sometimes.

I think this year, it'd be really cool if I can manage to have some kids produce a video of their evidence. That would be a lot of fun. The first year, I had some students working with the topic of immigration and one of the students' parents was actually super deep in immigration activism. She knew an immigration lawyer and another student actually had his parent show up and the lawyer interviewed his mom. It was completely in Spanish, but they spoke to her about what people can do for immigration. This all happened when Immigrations Customs Enforcement (ICE) was raiding homes. They also passed out flyers of what you can do when ICE shows up at your door. They videotaped it, and showed the video to the class.

I would also really like to follow through this year with any group that I can and give them as much support as I can to help them implement their project at lunch. Whether it be a booth, a presentation, role playing at lunch, anything.

Dr. Hays: Okay, if you had to put a number on it, what percentage of students do you feel were actively engaged in this work?

Mr. Muñoz: Off the top of my head, a solid 80–85 percent. And the ones that were left out were left in the dust. And that may be because of their own reasons. They have other issues going on in their lives that they really feel like they cannot even handle on their own. So, having to take on a whole other issue was just a lot for them. That's something I'm trying to work on. I need to understand when students have actual issues in their lives that they don't know how to deal with, and then I bring upon them another issue that I'd like them to take on, and that can be difficult.

Dr. Hays: Interestingly, one of the things I've found in all the research is that most of the kids who choose to focus on mental illness, they almost all have experienced it.

Mr. Muñoz: Have experience with it in some sense. Their family.

Dr. Hays: Yes—they say that they identify because they themselves have it. Every student I've interviewed has said that they have mental illness, that's why they pick the topic. But every one of those students additionally, all they've done for their plan is raise awareness. That's it. No one has done a tangible, "I'm going to take some sort of problem-solving step." And I'm wondering if it's the same with your students. They are in it and they can't figure out . . .

Mr. Muñoz: It's just too much of an issue for him to deal with. Yeah. It's just too big. So maybe this time around if I try to assign a student that I know who has actual issues with the actual topic, maybe I could just emphasize that this isn't something that's going to solve your life. This is going to be a step toward figuring out what's going on with what you're dealing with to better understand it, instead of trying to save the world. Maybe this year I can definitely emphasize that, so kids don't feel so overwhelmed or feel like it's pointless. Because that might be another factor that contributes to their lack of motivation.

Dr. Hays: I'm wondering if maybe for some kids, it's too raw and too real to read about an issue they are personally dealing with, and maybe it would be better for them to focus on something different.

Mr. Muñoz: Yeah and sometimes people deal with difficult issues by laughing about it or joking about it, not taking it seriously. They want to joke about it so they don't have to deal with it as much as they need to. Because it's just how they cope. At the same time, they need to be exposed, they need to know, they need to be aware that other people deal with the same things you deal with so that you can understand that even though it's not a common thing, it's not unheard of. You can speak to other people that have dealt with this issue and you can relate to other people that have dealt with this issue. So, I think it would be really helpful this year to make sure I emphasize that idea and make them understand that it's important that they find something to relate with.

Dr. Hays: What piece of advice do you have for someone who wants to do this work?

Mr. Muñoz: Be open to ideas and be supportive to ideas, no matter what a kid brings to the table. It's obviously important to them. You need to defend that student as much as you can. I regret not being able to support students the way I should have two years ago.

A second one is to just give in to the process. Let kids work and they're going to produce if they want to produce. And if you need to motivate them to produce a little more, then do it, but ultimately kids are going to produce what they want to produce. And you should support them.

One huge thing I gathered from this project was that when kids do this project they can understand how to be a better human, how to be a better citizen, and how to connect with other people to rally support for issues. Because a lot of the times we're in our own holes and we're sort of losing that factor that makes us more compassionate toward other people or empathetic. And I really think it's important that people learn that because there's so much strain today about different ideas. We can't live like everything's black and white or red and blue. Kids need to be able to value each other and other people and take issues seriously while learning that they are capable of dealing with these issues.

Dr. Hays: Thank you for your time and energy!

TEACHER 2: MS. NEFF

Ms. Neff had just completed her sixth year of teaching at the time of this interview, which puts her past the danger zone of burnout, but still in the early stages of a long career. She believes adolescents are far more capable than society lets on, and her teaching is student-centered. She has a calm persona that allows students room to express themselves and be comfortable in her room. She is always thoughtful in her reactions to the students and situations in her school and classroom. The idea of pushing against the system was appealing to her, and she loved this curriculum. At an National Council of Teachers of English conference, she told the audience that this curriculum changed her entire approach to teaching, and she has received a great deal of positive feedback about her teaching as a direct result of this curriculum.

Since she has now led her students through this curriculum four times, she has curated some amazing stories about her students. There are some wonderful ideas contained in this interview about the types of ways students might take up this work that I hope you will find as amazing as I did.

Dr. Hays: The first question that I am curious about, that we haven't really talked about before, is: Do you feel like in any way that this curriculum has changed the way that you view your students?

Ms. Neff: Oh man. I would say that the curriculum helps me get to know my students. It definitely changes the way I view them in terms of being learners, because a lot of students come in and I'm not really sure what type of learner they are. Then all of a sudden we start on this YA unit, and they become these self-motivated individuals who want to actually immerse themselves in meaningful work. That changes my whole perception that these kids want to have meaningful learning experiences, instead of the typical traditional method of learning English.

Dr. Hays: Can you talk a little bit more about that? In terms of that juxtaposition between when you say meaningful versus traditional, typical English?

Ms. Neff: Traditional, typical English, okay. We're all going to read this novel together. Here's a study guide, and here's questions you're going to need to answer. Then here's an essay now that we're finished reading the book. That day is usually like, "Oh write about the theme, or analyze a character." Some sort of literary analysis and then, "Oh, if there was a movie, let's watch the movie now."

When I did that in the past with my classes, I would reach some students. With the YAL, I would say 90 percent of them get into it. There's always a couple who are just apathetic through the whole thing, and they don't get as much out of it as others. It's like the whole engagement thing with the YAL is this more natural, organic engagement right away. Instead of this feeling like ritualistic compliance, it's actual real, authentic engagement.

Dr. Hays: That's awesome. What do you think the students are finding in it that makes them want to be so engaged?

Ms. Neff: Well, they're discovering things about themselves and about their groups that they work with. They're learning about what they have in common with other students in the class. I've even had some of them write me little happy grams, or just tell me face to face, "Ms. Neff, I'm really glad that we're able to talk about real issues in the world that matter. Instead of just reading the book, and not really talking about it or writing an essay."

Dr. Hays: I love that.

Ms. Neff: In turn, it just creates an environment of respect and rapport, not only for me and the students, but amidst the students. For example, in my regular class, I have thirty-four students and it's probably my most challenging class, as far as management through the school day. I have some kids in there who are immature. They shocked me toward the end of the semester when the antidefamation league (ADL) came in. They came in to work with my sophomores and they did this activity that opened up the discussion for students sharing very personal stories about themselves. The activities started out with them getting cards that all had something written on them that was either considered an advantage or disadvantage.

For example, one of the cards was like, "My mom is an alcoholic and my father's in prison." "I'm gay, I am transgender." Things like that. Students opened up about the cards that they got, but some of the cards that they got directly related to who they were or experiences they have had. They shared those experiences out with each other, and I was just blown away that they did that. Because we're talking about students who hardly said a word all semester, except to their little circle group.

Then all of a sudden they're sharing out with this little class. The whole class was very mature, and composed. And they listened to each other and showed this compassion. It was just absolutely incredible, and I can't help but think, had I not done that YAL unit and we had not already touched on the topic, and allowed that space for students to open up, that probably wouldn't have happened.

Dr. Hays: Wow! That's great. Did the ADL people say anything about your class's reception of the activity as compared to other classes?

Ms. Neff: Yeah, they actually went to the teacher who runs the club here on campus. She told me that they came to her and said that it was the best class that they had worked with all semester.

Dr. Hays: That's so awesome.

Ms. Neff: Yeah, I was blown away.

Dr. Hays: I love that. Okay. You've now worked through this curriculum four times. I'm sure that you know so much more than I do about what to consider, and what to think about as you're getting ready to set it up. Things like potential issues that might crop up, or things that you should be wary of. Can you speak to that a little bit?

Ms. Neff: Potential issues?

Dr. Hays: Mm-hmm (affirmative), and also things organizationally too. I guess that's a twofold question.

Ms. Neff: Well, I didn't have a huge issue with organization. I actually felt like organizing was pretty easy.

Dr. Hays: Can you give a quick rundown of how you yourself organized it, what tools or tricks you've used?

Ms. Neff: I used Microsoft OneNote for organized materials for the unit. We've made it easy for students to access all their documents that they needed [through folders in OneNote]. I always introduced the interest survey at the beginning and then I put them into groups. The survey makes it easy to do that. I also limited the amount of people in each group to four this year. That's important if you have a big class. This year I have three of the sophomore classes; one class that was of seventeen students, a class of thirty-four, and a class of thirty-two. With the smaller class, I was able to have more groups of two and three. I think I had one group of four. That was kind of nice. I noticed that groups who were paired with less than four were more productive and there were less issues.

One of the issues I did run into is, because I'm pairing these kids based on their interests, not necessarily on their personalities or by their academic abilities, that one group of two butted heads. Their personalities did not jive. They were constantly arguing and bickering. I sat down with them two times, had a conversation with them about, "Hey, here's what has to happen. This is what I expect."

After those two times, things didn't get better. I had a final conversation with them. I said, "Okay, here's what's going to happen. Either I'm splitting you two up and you're going to work individually for the rest of the project, or I'm going to put you guys with a new group." Well, they didn't want to work by themselves. They wanted to work in a group. I ended up moving them into different groups, which meant that they had to get onboard with a new topic and a new project.

Dr. Hays: What were some of the other things to look out for?

Ms. Neff: Some of the other issues—I had a parent who emailed me concerned about her son being put in the environment group. She screened the book *Kingsley* and had some issues with the content, specifically the rape that occurs. She asked me to assign him a different book. What I did is, I sent her a list of all of the ones to choose from, but I did point out that out of all of those novels, the safest or most G-rated was *The Circuit* and *Breaking Through*. He ended up working with that group. It was interesting because this student comes from a white, very Christian family, and his group mates were all Hispanic and came from immigrant families.

Dr. Hays: So how did he do with that?

Ms. Neff: He definitely told me a couple of times that he learned a lot about the issue. He actually got really into the issue, especially when it came to the action piece project. He and the other male in the group became very, very close. They're really good friends now.

Dr. Hays: Oh, that's awesome.

Ms. Neff: It's funny because this semester, after the unit, I let them choose where they wanted to sit. They wanted to sit next to each other still.

Dr. Hays: Lifelong friendships being formed, I hope. My next question is, of all the projects that you've seen your students do, which one was maybe the most impactful?

Ms. Neff: Wow. Well, there were a lot.

Dr. Hays: Say the top five then, or whichever ones you were most excited about?

Ms. Neff: One of them was actually from this year, and there were two students who went and volunteered at a Welcome to America project. And I don't know if you're familiar with what that is, but it's an organization that helps rehome refugees. And they came back from doing that. . . . They did it on a Saturday, and so they came to class on Monday, and they were just like, "Oh my God, it was so awesome. I learned so much, and it was so much fun. And people were so nice. And I want to go back and do it every weekend."

They took everything that they did, and they went around to different classrooms on campus, and shared their experience.

Then there's another group who volunteered at My Starving Children, and they had the same experience. They were just blown away by how awesome it was. And I feel like students who actually get out and talk to people, work in the communities, and have an actual hands-on experience get so much more out of it.

Dr. Hays: Oh, that's an interesting observation. That's something I would agree with too, just thinking about my own experiences with my own students.

Ms. Neff: Yeah. The first year, a group of students put together a video montage, where they interviewed their peers about their experiences with racism. It was such a powerful and emotional video. I was crying, and people who watched it cried. It was just very eye opening, and it just . . . it made me sick to my stomach to hear these students' stories about how they were treated. But the good thing that came out of that was everyone who watched the video was able to relate and connect. And they were like, "Wow, I'm not the only one."

Dr. Hays: Right, yeah. Which is really powerful, I think, in a lot of ways.

Ms. Neff: Another group, this year, did a really cool project. It's the group who read *Sold*, the one on human trafficking. They actually set up an interview and talked to actual agents from Homeland Security.

Dr. Hays: Really?

Ms. Neff: Yeah. So, they conducted telephone interviews, which was a really good primary source, talking to one of the agents. And based on the information that they got, they learned that the target age group of children who are being trafficked are junior high school aged.

Dr. Hays: Oh wow.

Ms. Neff: The students set up this whole presentation at their junior high school. And they coordinated with one of the teachers, and the principal, and they spent an entire day at their junior high school educating students there.

Dr. Hays: That is so incredible. So, lots of amazing projects. So what would you say was your biggest takeaway? What did you find the most positive?

Ms. Neff: Just from the whole unit in general?

Dr. Hays: Yeah, from the whole curriculum in general, yeah.

Ms. Neff: It opens up doors to new opportunities and experiences, not just in the classroom, but outside of the classroom. It allows them. . . . It creates this awesome classroom environment, where we can talk about actual important issues that are going on, that affect them, and that they actually care about.

Dr. Hays: That's awesome.

Ms. Neff: And that, to me is. . . . It doesn't happen every day. It's so important to these kids, you know, it's actually like being high school students. I've just never seen anything like it, or experienced anything like it. And I don't think they have either, in any of their classes.

Dr. Hays: Thank you so much for your time and wisdom, Ms. Neff.

STUDENT EXPERIENCE: ISAIAH

Isaiah was a seventh grade student at the time of this interview and was a student in one of the other seventh grade teacher's classes. Isaiah is an outspoken young man who drew my attention in class every time I visited for his positive and enthusiastic participation. He is the type of person that someone might call an old soul, in that he was thoughtful about the purpose behind things, and seemed much wiser than one might expect a seventh grader to be at some points, while simultaneously lapsing into the ridiculousness with his peers in other times. In this interview, he shares his experience with developing an action plan to center on the environment.

The action plan that he and his group created was an Instagram account The Impacters, who claims to be "a group that brings awareness to Ecological Issues." They posted interviews with teachers and students from their school that showcased their interviewees' level of understanding around the environment and humans' impact on the environment, and they continued to post images, memes, and facts about the environment into July of that year.

Dr. Hays: Okay. So this is Isaiah who read . . . who read. . . . What did you read?

Isaiah: Flushed. Yeah, *Flush*.

Dr. Hays: Okay. If you would give a brief summary of the book, that would be super awesome.

Isaiah: Okay, so the book is about this kid, Isaiah, and his parents are in the middle of . . . well, they were getting ready to get divorced, because Isaiah's father was trying to fight against a problem with trash and waste being dumped in the ocean. So his father got imprisoned. And, basically, Isaiah is trying to prove that the reason his father sunk the boat was true.

Dr. Hays: Okay. Perfect. All right. How did you feel about it? You can be honest. There's no right or wrong.

Isaiah: At first, it was kind of boring. But it got more interesting in the middle.

Dr. Hays: Okay. Awesome. Very cool. So what prompted you to choose the issue of environmentalism?

Isaiah: I've just always . . . I've always been intrigued with this issue because it's a serious issue that's not really. . . . People don't really think it's important, but every [piece of] trash that's dropped each day—that can be something that we could just throw away in the trashcan or something like that.

Dr. Hays: Okay. I feel like you've sort of started to talk about it, but the next question is, how do you feel like the issue relates to your own life? How is it relevant? How do you see it mattering to you?

Isaiah: Well, because my family is really big with that. We've always . . . my mom has always taught us to recycle and things like that. I mean even if we weren't taught, I would still do that. But I think growing up in a family where it's important to recycle and care about the environment, I think that has a big impact.

Dr. Hays: So are there any of the characters in the book, any of them at all, that you feel like you, maybe, are like, "Oh, I'm kind of like that."

Isaiah: Yeah. Isaiah. Because he fights for what he believes in and that's something that I do. Even if it's not this issue, any other issue where anything, I believe in or anything I feel is right, I'm going to speak my mind. So, that's basically what he did, by trying to show that his father was innocent.

Dr. Hays: Awesome. Do you feel like you are more or less knowledgeable about the environment after reading the novel?

Isaiah: I think I did get some information, but, mostly, I did know most of the stuff before this. Because my mom's a teacher, so I know a lot about that stuff, in general.

Dr. Hays: So then that kind of leads into the next question. Within this particular project, you read the novel, you did the lit circles in groups, you did research and you have to do a presentation. Right? And then the action plan? And then, of course, you have your own experience of those things. Which do you think taught you the most about those issues?

Isaiah: I think it's where we had to do our action. Because we interviewed people and we asked them questions about the environment. And the purpose of that was to show how little people know about this issue because not a lot of people knew about it. They had no idea about it. And I feel like people thought that was a good idea because after we did that, a whole bunch of Instagram pages, and everything, really has popped up.

Dr. Hays: Oh, really?

Isaiah: Yeah. So, I think doing that interview was, it showed how little people knew about this issue. That was the point of it.

Dr. Hays: So what do you think you can do beyond the Instagram page you guys started? Do you have future goals for that besides just spreading awareness, or—?

Isaiah: Well, I feel like . . . I mean, there's some things that you can do, like picking up trash, which I know that's not going to help a lot. But still, if you like community service, which the Builder's Club do, like they've done before, they've gone out and picked up trash and stuff like that. I feel like if you just do little things like that, then it can add up, like not dumping trash on the ground or just recycling. Stuff like that. I think that would help.

Dr. Hays: Do you feel like this project will make a change?

Isaiah: Umm, yeah, I feel like it will make a change because. . . . Well, showing . . . I mean, I know like an Instagram page, I mean that's not gonna make a huge deal, but showing people how little, like your classmates or your *teachers* even, or people that are around you, know about this issue, I feel like showing them that shows that not a lot of people know about this issue and, yeah.

Dr. Hays: Is there anything else that you can think of that might help me understand what you were thinking about when you did this project, the unit plan. What was the process like? Did everybody work well together? Was it okay?

Isaiah: Okay, so at first, I was kind of bummed because not a lot of other groups didn't all get together [and create a plan]. But our classmates and our teachers told us that we made [a topic] that's not really fun, fun. [The environment is] something not a lot of students would like, something that students wouldn't think is interesting, and something that is like not really important to people [Then they told us] "You made it fun and we found a way to make it like people would be interested in it."

Dr. Hays: That's awesome.

Isaiah: Yeah, it was lots of fun doing this.

Dr. Hays: Do you feel like you got closer just with your group or do you feel like you got close with the whole class?

Isaiah: The whole class. Because, I mean, it's fun because everybody is talking. I mean, because you get to interact with people and I feel like you being able to do that, just changes a lot of things for a lot of people.

Dr. Hays: That's very cool. Was there any particular thing that you liked the best?

Isaiah: I think working on the plan was probably the best because our thing, it was. . . . We were actually going to do something. At the assembly, we were going to talk about it. That was our first thing. And then it was an Instagram page and interviewing people—we were just going to interview people and put it up in the assembly. But, Mr. Frost had the idea to combine them. Because I feel like talking to someone, and just interacting with them, can make someone's day.

Dr. Hays: Yes. Yeah, absolutely. I love it. In terms of the actual curriculum, are there any suggestions that you have for the teachers next year?

Isaiah: I mean, they gave us enough time, but I feel like for some things, I felt it was a little squeezed in.

Dr. Hays: Okay. What was that?

Isaiah: I mean, for me, it was fine. But some of the students, it was like, with the planning, with all the planning, because it takes some people longer to plan, so I feel like that was a little squeezed. And I don't think they gave us enough time for that. I mean we were fine with it because we had already figured out. . . . We had already brainstormed before we were on that step. But I feel like people didn't think about it, beforehand, like we did. So I feel like if we had a little more time with the groups, then it would be a lot easier.

Dr. Hays: Okay. To come up with the action plan?

Isaiah: Yeah.

Dr. Hays: Now do you think it's more, like, you need more time after the fact? Because I feel like you guys have done a pretty good job of having time to interview and get interviews posted.

Isaiah: Yeah, because we started planning way, way ahead. So, and they just started, probably, yesterday. . . . So, I feel like if we start a little earlier in the year, and then like—

Dr. Hays: So you have time to do the action.

Isaiah: Yeah. Because some people just barely started. And I feel like, when they feel like they have to rush it's not going to be as good.

Dr. Hays: Do you think you'd still do your action plan if your class had moved on? For example if they had done this during third quarter instead of at the end of the year, would you continue?

Isaiah: Oh, yeah, definitely. I think if you did this third or second or whatever quarter, I feel like it'd be. . . . People would still want to do it. Because, I mean, I think it does make more sense that we're doing it in fourth quarter because of how we have all the other books and stuff like that. But I feel like it would be a lot more fun if we did it in third quarter or something like that.

Dr. Hays: So would you recommend that your teacher do it again?

Isaiah: Yeah, definitely. Yeah, because I feel like everybody had a blast doing this because everybody was working together and just talking and just communicating. I feel like that just worked 100 percent. And even if you don't know these people, I feel like you get 100 percent closer with them.

Dr. Hays: Thank you, Isaiah.

Isaiah: You're welcome.

The common thread throughout all of these interviews is that the action plan and the ability for students to be independent creators and teams was a powerful and crucial part of the process. I think it is clear from these voices from the field that this curriculum can be powerful and engaging for both students and teachers alike. In Isaiah's words, "I feel like this just worked 100 percent," and I hope you are looking forward to your own stories from the field.

Appendix
Books for Social Justice Issues

The following books are based upon the topics that students identified over the past several years, although it is certainly not exhaustive.

MIDDLE SCHOOL BOOK IDEAS

Racism

Stella by Starlight, *Sharon M. Draper*

Stella is a novel about a young girl who lives in the segregated South in 1932. Stella experiences some people who are quite pleasant, and others who are less so. Stella writes about her memories of racism and discrimination that are further fueled by the reappearance of the Ku Klux Klan, and her goal to be brave enough to stand up for herself and her family.

This novel is fairly accessible to younger students, although the time period makes it a little more difficult for students to relate the events to contemporary times. If you are concerned about pushback from the community, this may be a good resource to introduce the idea of racism to some students. It might take some work to help students draw comparisons between what was happening then in terms of intimidation and what sorts of events might occur today, in order to identify how they might take action around this issue.

Poverty

Crenshaw, *Katherine Applegate*

Crenshaw by Katherine Applegate focuses on the experiences of fourth grader, Jackson, whose parents have lost their home. The boy examines his situation through a scientific eye, and also deals with his issues through long conversations with Crenshaw, his former imaginary cat friend. The novel is honest, but hopeful in the end, and presents a complex examination of homelessness in a way sure to generate empathy.

This novel is great for students from eight years and up and is a fairly quick read. While the idea of an imaginary friend may seem a bit "kiddish," the topic itself is very mature and handled quite well. This novel has a contemporary setting, and shows a good family that has fallen on hard times. In this story, the main character has a supportive and loving family. Students who are homeless and have different home situations may struggle with the depiction of this idyllic family.

Immigration

The Circuit *and* Breaking Through, *Francisco Jimenez*

These two memoir novellas tell the early story of Francisco's journey as a migrant worker in the United States. It depicts the grueling life of a field worker from the perspective of a young boy who just wants to help his family but is forced to do things he feels are beneath him, such as babysitting his infant brother in the car while his parents work. It also details his experiences on his first venture into American schools, and the struggles and difficulties he goes through as someone who does not speak the language but is desperate to get an education.

This book is powerful for people whose families have experienced this path to American citizenship. One student who read it said that it felt validating to see that her family stories were true. It also helps to give perspective for people who only hear the tagline that immigrants are taking jobs away from people. Seeing exactly what work these people are doing, and the struggles they go through, can humanize what is often de-humanized in the news. This book is a very easy read, which is why it is a good idea to pair both the first and second memoirs in the series together for this group.

The Distance Between Us, *Reyna Grande*

Reyna Grande wrote her own migration story, but it begins from the perspective of the young daughter who is left behind. This story is also autobiographical, as Jimenez's is, and she recounts her experiences missing the father who left her and her mother behind to make a better life for himself, and by extension, them, in America. The novel details the added struggles and strains that this grasp at upward mobility places on families who are torn apart.

This book is a little more mature than the Jimenez books, and some students may find it difficult to get through. An added bonus is that this book is readily available in Spanish, which may make it more accessible for some students. This book was used with great success in a local high school's book club for both students and their families, which created a strong sense of community between the families and the school.

Drug Abuse

Hey Kiddo, *Jason Krosoczka*

This graphic novel depicts a protagonist who lives with his grandparents because his mother is a drug addict. It details the complex relationship he has with his grandparents and mother, as well as the difficult feelings he grapples with. He ultimately turns to art as a way to manage his feelings and explore them.

This book is an easy one to read in terms of comprehension. There were students who read it and felt a little unsettled by it due to the novel's realistic depiction of a life similar to their own. It also helps students to understand that their own conflicting feelings about the adults in their lives who make mistakes are normal. While students enjoyed the reading, they struggled to find an idea for their action plan from this book. For many of them, they felt like the book already was the solution, and they didn't know what else they'd address from that. They may need encouragement to think through the project more creatively after reading this novel, in terms of looking to see how the protagonist deals with his issues by himself.

Women's Rights

Hidden Figures, *Margot Lee Shetterly*

This story focuses on five black women who played a major part in the United States' Space Race victory. This book is set during the civil rights movement, and tells the tale of the "Human Computers" along with the added struggles they experienced due to their race, in addition to their gender. Typically, the early stories of our space exploration focus on the astronauts who took the flights, but this story showcases the women without whom the rockets would have never left the ground.

There is a great deal of math discussion in the original book, which may be daunting for students who are less math oriented. This book also comes in a young readers edition, which is a touch more accessible. Additionally, there is a picture book version, illustrated by Winifred Conkling and Laura Freeman, for the even younger reader.

Amal Unbound, *Aisha Saeed*

This story centers on a young Pakistani girl whose sole dream is to become a teacher. As the eldest daughter, she is made to stay home from school to take care of her young siblings, which is upsetting, although she still manages to find ways to learn. Unfortunately, she has an accidental run-in with the corrupt family who act as the landlords of the village. As a result of this run-in, she is forced to work as their servant to pay off her family's debt.

This book was a Goodreads Choice Award for middle grade and children's literature in 2018, and is accessible to moderately young readers. There is indentured servitude and some violence, but nothing significant. While this novel does focus on a lack of women's rights, it may be difficult for students to see Amal's struggles as similar to issues that American girls and women deal with, so you may want to be cognizant of that before assigning this book.

Social Media Awareness

Click'd, *Tamara Ireland*

This novel focuses on a young girl, Allie Navarro, who spends her summer at CodeGirls summer camp and develops a new friendship-building app. The app aligns people's interests, and users go off on a search to try to find the new friend they never knew existed. Not only is the app incredibly successful at bringing Allie's school together, it looks likely to also help her win a computer coding competition against one of her least favorite people in the school, Nathan. Unfortunately, a glitch in the app starts to spread people's darkest secrets and threatens to ruin more lives than it helps. The only way Allie can fix this is by enlisting the help of people who know as much as she does, and that means working with her competition, which will certainly mean losing the contest. Will she do the right thing at the risk of losing the big prize?

This book is a quick, easy-to-read book, although the issues that can come about from dumping too much personal information into social media were somewhat downplayed according to students who read the book. They felt the book focused more on the relationships in real life than it did on the technology within the book. This book would be good for people who specifically want to think about the personal relationships that are helped or broken due to social media, although it may not be good for students who are interested in examining the potentially nefarious aspects of technology.

In Real Life, *Cory Doctorow*

This graphic novel focuses on a young girl who joins a multiplayer-role-playing game called Coarsegold Online. She loves it because she is able to be a leader, a fighter, and a hero in this virtual world. The protagonist ends up befriending a poor Chinese kid who is breaking the rules of the online platform, and while the protagonist Anda is initially opposed to his behavior, she realizes that the rules of society become much more blurred when someone's real life is at stake.

Corey Doctorow states that the book is about the political, economic, and social choices we make on a daily basis. Additionally, he focuses on the real life social justice issues behind the online games and virtual world. There are some potential concerns here about the main character acting like a "white savior" and stepping in and helping the poor Chinese kid she meets online. For your students who enjoy graphic novels and video games, however, this would be a great introduction to considering the social justice implications of some of our daily behaviors.

Domestic Abuse/Violence

Ghost, *Jason Reynolds*

In this story, Castle Crenshaw, or Ghost, began running the night his dad shot at him and his mom and never stopped. While he saw himself as a basketball player, he ends up running against a track star, and ultimately beating him. This causes the coach to sit up and take notice, and ultimately recruit him to be on the team. The story is about how Ghost tries to outrun his past, but he can't quite escape it.

This novel does not solely focus or center on domestic abuse, although the story does begin that way. Instead this novel focuses more on the trauma that Ghost experiences, the way he lashes out, and the importance of his coach in his life. Students enjoy reading this book, but may need support in seeing how domestic violence contributed to Ghost's behaviors and how to come up with an action plan to address issues that arise from reading this book.

Long Way Down, *Jason Reynolds*

This novel set in verse focuses on a young man, Will, who has set out to take revenge on his brother's murder. The story is set in an elevator and lasts for as long as it takes him to ride the elevator down. At each stop, a different ghost steps on the elevator to expose him to the very real consequences of gun violence, and the vicious cycle at play in Will's life.

Students will read this book quickly, and while violence is not specifically depicted in the book, it is the centerpiece of the story. There are myriad ideas to focus on here, including laws around gun violence, the systemic nature of violence in some communities, and the potentially debilitating effects of living up to expected norms. When Jason Reynolds talks to kids about the book, he always asks them if they want to know what happened at the end, because it is a cliff-hanger. They always respond that they do, and he always tells them that it is ultimately their choice to decide what happens, because it depends solely on their own actions. This is exactly what students should realize from reading this novel, and it lends itself well to the development of an action plan.

Mental Health/Suicide

Cut, *Patricia McCormick*

Cut is a novel about a young girl who is placed in an institution after her substitute school nurse discovers she is cutting herself. In the beginning of the novel, Callie, the protagonist, is not speaking to anyone at all. This gives her time to observe others, which allows for an in-depth look at multiple types of "issues" represented by her fellow group members. Over the course of the book, we discover that many of the girls have a paradoxical sense of powerlessness, yet feel as though they are the cause of trauma or difficulties in other people's lives.

This novel is particularly interesting in that the support Callie needs is depicted as being absolutely unavailable, but when Callie ultimately reaches out to that person, they do reenter the picture. This book shows quite clearly how different people handle things in different ways, and their reaction to you may not be a direct result of your behavior. Additionally, the book focuses on the fact that the individual must find the strength to fight their issue internally, as nothing on the outside can ultimately save the person.

Environment

Flush, *Carl Hiaasen*

This book is about Noah proving that the local casino boat is polluting the harbor by flushing raw sewage into the ocean. He is trying to pick up where his father left off, since his father is in jail for sinking the boat. With some innovation and help from his friends, Noah comes up with an idea to prove that the boat owner is doing bad things.

This book is an easy one to read, and is pretty straight forward. Students who have read this book see the clear example of how the sewage is harming the environment, although several students struggled to extrapolate this mystery pollution to the larger environmental pollution they tend to want to think about. It may be helpful to show them other examples of environmental activism in addition to this book.

Hoot, *Carl Hiaasen*

This novel is a coming-of-age story that ultimately relies on the ingenuity and determination of a group of adolescents to protect the environment from a construction project. An endangered owl family's home is going to be destroyed if a local pancake house finishes completion. Roy and his newfound friends come up with a variety of ways to try to stop the construction of the building.

While this novel ultimately reveals the environment as the focus of their efforts, it spends a great deal of time focusing on the power of adolescents to come together to enact change. This would be a good book to discuss the power of young people coming together as they fight larger power structures, although it may also be a good idea to address the illegal nature of some of their moves, and how they are not entirely successful.

Bullying/Peer Pressure

Blubber, *Judy Blume*

This classic novel focuses on the bullying of Linda, who completes a book report about whales, and ends up being given the unfortunate nickname of Blubber by the school's mean girl. Judy Blume wrote the novel in response to her own daughter's bullying experiences, after realizing that at the time novels about bullying did not exist.

While this is a book that has been around for years, it doesn't make the storyline any less impactful. And in fact, due to lower levels of supervision in the 1970s, there are moments where the bullying may seem even more severe in real life than it may be in today's school spaces. This book also espouses the idea that the victim is better off talking to trusted adults than dealing with the situation on their own.

Human Trafficking

Sold, *Patricia McCormick*

This novel focuses on the story of Lakshmi, who is a thirteen-year-old girl living in a small hut in the mountains of Nepal. While they are desperately poor, her family finds joy in the small aspects of life until their house is destroyed by a storm. Her father tells her that she must take a job, and she happily goes to India with a stranger where she is told she will be a maid to earn money to send to her family. She discovers very quickly that she has actually been sold into prostitution, and she learns to endure, which can be counted as a triumph.

The novel does have a happy ending, although it is definitely difficult to get through. Students who read this novel found the storyline incredibly important, though, and were glad to have read the book. It does not necessarily directly correlate with an American vision of human trafficking; however, the emotional impact of the writing allowed students to see the power and importance of this story. As a teacher, you will want to be prepared for the chapters where she is assaulted so you can support your students through them if they need an extra ear to talk to, or simply to forewarn them about what is to come. While the writing is not graphic, it is powerful. This novel would work well for both middle school and upper grades.

HIGH SCHOOL BOOK IDEAS

Refugee/Immigration

The Good Braider, by Terry Farish

This free-verse novel centers on Viola's journey from war-torn Sudan, to Cairo, and ultimately to Portland, Maine. Viola and her mother flee Sudan when their way of life is threatened in significant ways. The novel depicts the journey to Cairo and what it is like to live in refugee tents with no idea what might become of you in ways that are both a stark and beautiful depiction of humanity. Ultimately, they end up in America, where the behavior of the girls Viola meets is in bitter contrast with her mother's expectations. She struggles to navigate the reality of becoming a part of America while also holding onto her Sudanese heritage.

This book is well written, and does a beautiful job of depicting the struggles and strength of refugees who must flee their homes. Students who read this will have a strong understanding of how it is that someone would pick up and move to another country with not much more than the clothes on their back, and they may also have a more nuanced understanding of why some people don't immediately want to assimilate to become more "American" in all ways. This will also allow readers to consider different ways they might support refugees in their action plan, as it also shows the reality of trying to make one's way in a new land.

Refugee, by Alan Gratz

This book is a novel that focuses on three different individuals who are all fleeing. While their stories occur decades apart (1930s, 1994, and 2015), Gratz tells the stories in tandem, showing some of the similarities between their stories. Josef, a Jewish boy fleeing Nazi Germany, is the first storyline. Isabel is a Cuban girl who sets off on a raft to America. Mahmoud is a Syrian boy traveling toward Europe. Gratz does a great job of showing the parallels of their stories and ultimately tying them all together.

This novel is very well written as well as being a fascinating study of humanity over the past seventy years. While many students are familiar with events from World War II and the Holocaust, many of them are not aware of the fact that these types of events are continuing to occur around the world.

This novel showcases this parallel reality in powerful ways. The novel does not address their arrival in much detail, so students may need support in thinking through how they might take action locally, if that is what they are trying to do.

Muslim Discrimination

Does My Head Look Big in This?, *Randa Abdel-Fattah*

This novel focuses on sixteen-year-old Amal who makes a decision to wear her hijab full time as a way of embracing her faith. Her friends and family warn her against doing it due to their fear of retaliation against her, but she feels that a piece of material shouldn't matter that much. She experiences both discrimination and acceptance throughout the novel, ultimately learning about her own faith and relationship with her friends and family.

This book is a good, nuanced example of what it means to embrace a faith that is not a part of the majority group. The exploration of one girl's experiences, coupled with the firsthand perspective of how she deals with it, may give readers some insight into what it means to try to embrace one's faith in obvious ways, which may lead them to think about more nuanced action plans.

Racial Equality

All American Boys, *Jason Reynolds and Brendan Kiely*

This novel covers two parallel lives that intersect through a horrific event. Rashad, a black male, is accused of trying to steal a woman's purse, and is beaten so severely by a police officer that he ends up in the hospital. Quinn, a white male, is a witness to the beating from afar, and knows the police officer. Over the course of the novel, the two boys are both trying to figure out how to navigate this reality from their own perspectives, and ultimately raise their voices together.

This novel is particularly powerful in that it shows the police brutality and treatment, of a kid who is very much an "all-American boy", from his viewpoint as a victim, as well as from the viewpoint of a white boy who recognizes that something isn't right but is caught up in a sense of loyalty to the police officer initially. The story unfolds in a way that gently eases the student who doesn't think racism exists anymore into the storyline without causing him or her to become defensive. While there are many good books that discuss the very real inequities that people of color experience in America, this differs in that it pulls you through a white boy's growing realization of that fact in compelling ways. This book truly is a conversation starter.

Gender Equality

The Boston Girl, *Anita Diamante*

This novel focuses on the journey of a young Jewish woman who immigrated to America in the early 1900s. It is told as a memory from the grandmother to her granddaughter about her experiences at not only expanding past her parents' cultural expectations but also expanding her role as a woman in America.

This book is easy to read, and examines Addie's journey at trying to make a name for herself in America. The students who read the book did enjoy it, although as the novel is set in the early 1900s, the students struggled to draw connections between then and now. It may be a good idea to help students identify similar, more contemporary examples of what Addie goes through during the reading so they can find more to connect with up front.

LGBTQ

Openly Straight, *Bill Konigsberg*

This novel takes an incredibly creative approach to the typical coming out story in that the primary character, Rafe, is actively trying to "go back in." He is "the" gay student at his small-town high school, and his mom is the president of the local parent group intended to support LGBTQ students. As a result, Rafe is forced to be the spokesperson for the LGBTQ community, which is a role he is not comfortable filling. He convinces his parents to allow him to go to a boarding school so he can "be straight." His ability to hide a core aspect of himself is less realistic than he anticipates, however, and the novel discusses an interesting and unique aspect of LGBTQ issues coupled with identity issues.

Readers who have a limited understanding of the difficulties and complexities of what it means to be LGBTQ within a predominantly straight community will be exposed to a nuanced depiction of the internal struggles many students go through. This book is appropriate for high school students who understand relationships but may have some misunderstanding around LGBTQ relationships.

Every Day, *David Levithan*

This novel focuses on A, who is a character who wakes up every single day in a new person's body. This has been their existence all their life, and they don't know any different. Levithan describes the sensation A has when waking up in a drug-addicted body, and how painful it is to go through withdrawal for a day, as well as what it's like to be sad at the end of a great day because the next day could bring terror and difficulties. In this novel, A ends up waking up in a boy's body, and the boy happens to have an amazing girlfriend. Through a series of happy accidents, A ends up connecting with the girlfriend in multiple ways, and their very complicated relationship develops.

This novel is particularly interesting because it really explores what love might mean, and whether or not one's physical body is a limitation for love, or simply a carrier for love. While the character does not necessarily examine the ways that a person might have to deal with their sexuality in a highly public way, it does explore how someone else might deal with their love for someone who doesn't fit the societal norm of what they expect.

Poverty

Eleanor & Park, *Rainbow Rowell*

This novel focuses on a young girl, Eleanor, who suffers from significant poverty, and uses avoidant and antagonistic behavior as a form of self-protection. She meets Park on the bus, who reluctantly allows her to sit in his seat so she can avoid being bullied, and they bond over comic books and music. Eleanor and Park's relationship is tenuous at best, due to the fragile nature of their power as adolescents. While Park attempts to be the savior for Eleanor, he is ultimately unable to do this.

Readers who have a limited understanding of the crippling aspects of poverty will be exposed to a character who is smart and creative/innovative yet cannot escape poverty regardless of how hard she works. This book does have a few words that may be deemed inappropriate by sensitive readers, and there is suggestion of verbal abuse and sexual harassment, although nothing is graphically depicted in the novel.

Abuse

Chinese Handcuffs, *Chris Crutcher*

This story focuses on Dillon and Jennifer who are athletes and friends who are grappling with super-size problems. In the novel, Dillon sees his brother commit suicide, and Jennifer is being molested by her stepfather, after having been previously molested by her father. Together, the two of them find strength to confront their issues.

This novel is not for the faint of heart. There is a significant amount of language in the novel that may offend many, and the content is graphic. When it discusses abuse, it is covering myriad types of abuse, and students who read this will need to be mature, and prepared for the gritty realities of these situations. It is important to note that Crutcher works as a family therapist, and his primary goal for writing the books he does is to help students who are going through these horrific experiences see that they are not alone. In fact, through this book, he discovered that one of his own family members had experienced some of the trauma Crutcher writes about, and she thought that he had written the book for her specifically. While this book is an incredible and powerful read, it may feel contrived to people who have had no experience with these types of abuse, and over the top. I do want to share that Crutcher has worked with people who have had lives as difficult and traumatic as the ones he depicts, so you may have students who need to hear this story, even if you are not aware of it.

Mental Health

It's Kind of a Funny Story, *Ned Vizzini*

This story was a pseudo-autobiographical novel that encompasses the five-day period in Ned Vizzini's life where he spent time in a psychiatric ward. The novel's main character, Craig, is a perfectionist and does everything in his power to get into an elite private high school that will virtually guarantee his life success, or so he thinks. The debilitating nature of trying to be perfect ultimately pushes him to consider jumping off a bridge, although he has the ability to recognize this as problematic and signs himself into a mental institution, where he makes an unlikely group of friends, and ultimately is able to find a way through the darkness.

This novel not only explores Craig's own issues but also exposes the issues that other people are experiencing, providing a nuanced glimpse into mental illness. The students I interviewed who have read this found a sense of company in the writing, as many of them chose the book because they felt as though they had their own mental illness to deal with. I do recommend this book with some hesitancy, however, as Ned Vizzini did ultimately succumb to his own illness in 2013. While the novel itself ends on a hopeful note, the same cannot be said for the author himself.

Environment

Kingsley, *Carolyn O'Neal*

This novel is set in a dystopian future in which a virus has attacked and killed all bees and ultimately kills all males. The main character Kingsley is the last male on earth, and he has a crush on his best friend, Amanda, although both of them are ultimately the pawns of their overbearing and controlling mothers. The first part of the novel focuses on their attempts to figure out what is going on. A third of the way into the novel, the setting changes to forty years into the future when there has been a complete collapse of society and the world is even scarier than when Kingsley and Amanda were trying to figure things out.

The novel is a bit unusual in its structure and organization, although students who are interested in science fiction and the environment will do well with this book. There are some profanity and some disturbing sexual situations to be aware of, although none of them are described graphically, so you may want to keep that in mind as you are considering which students might want to read this.

Dry, *Neal Shusterman*

This novel is set in Southern California when the drought becomes so drastic that all water taps are shut off without warning. While the protagonist believes things will be okay at first, the rapidity of dehydration on a person's body causes the upper-middle-class suburban neighborhood to spiral into an apocalyptic nightmare within hours. The main character, Alyssa, has to make life and death decisions to save her brother's life when her parents don't return from a water-finding mission.

As someone who grew up in the Arizona desert and now resides in California, I found this particularly hard to read. The beginning premise of the novel rests on the idea that there have been water restrictions in place for years, although people tend to ignore them if they feel inconvenienced. I myself have grown up with these same restrictions, so it all felt a little more realistic than I would have liked. This novel does have some violence, although it is not described in particularly graphic detail. The book itself was coauthored by Neal Shusterman and his son, Jarrod, which does make the novel feel slightly different in tone from Neal's other novels, although still highly readable and engaging.

Technology

Feed, *M.T. Anderson*

This novel is set in the dystopian future, and almost every person has an internet advertising and information feed connected directly to their brains. While it may seem incredibly helpful to have access to that information, the normalization of the constant stimulation causes the adolescents in the novel to become overly reliant on the feed. It isn't until a number of the teens are hacked, and they are pulled off the feed for a bit that Titus meets Violet whose goal is to fight against the feed.

This novel is somewhat uncanny in how similar it is to some of our current realities, although some students may not see the correlation immediately. Much of the message of the novel comes through in satire, and the book exposes society's willingness to be controlled by capitalistic desires in many ways. As this book veers into science fiction, students may struggle to see the ways that they can apply the information to their daily experiences, although there are definitely correlations. In order to come up with an action plan, the readers will need to be creative in the way they think about this work.

Bullying

Yaqui Delgado Wants to Kick Your Ass, *Meg Medina*

This book centers on Piddy, a girl who has just started at a new high school and almost immediately draws the ire of Yaqui, who thinks Piddy is acting stuck up. While the bullying initially starts with words, it ultimately moves into the physical, and Piddy has to figure out how to cope without making things worse for herself.

The book is a realistic depiction of what bullying looks like for high school kids without ending in the stereotypical resolution of the bully being just as hurt, and them becoming friends. This book shows strong LatinX women who are a support system in and of themselves, which is critical when Piddy refuses to become a narc in order to deal with the situation. Many students will see their own experiences in this story, and it can be powerful to see how she ends up leaning on the resources she does have in positive ways.

Works Cited

Alsup, Janet. 2015. *Case for Teaching Literature in the Secondary School*. Taylor and Francis.
Anderson, M.T. 2002. *Feed*. Cambridge: Candlewick Press.
Applebee, Arthur N., Judith A. Langer, Martin Nystrand, and Adam Gamoran. 2003. "Discussion-Based Approaches to Developing Understanding: Classroom Instruction and Student Performance in Middle and High School English." *American Educational Research Journal* 40 (3): 685–730. https://doi.org/http://dx.doi.org/10.3102/00028312040003685.
Beach, Richard, Anthony Johnston, and Amanda Haertling Thein. 2015. *Identity-Focused ELA Teaching*. Taylor and Francis.
Bishop, Rudine Sims. 1990. "Windows and Mirrors: Children's Books and Parallel Cultures." *Illinois English Bulletin* 78 (1): 83.
Brabham, Edna Greene, and Susan Kidd Villaume. 2000. "Continuing Conversations about Literature Circles." *Reading Teacher* 54 (3): 278–80. http://content.ebscohost.com.ezproxy.webfeat.lib.ed.ac.uk/ContentServer.asp?T=P&P=AN&K=3743371&S=R&D=afh&EbscoContent=dGJyMMTo50SeqLM4y9f3OLCmr0qeprVSsqu4SreWxWXS&ContentCustomer=dGJyMPGprkmxprVMuePfgeyx43zx%5Cnhttp://ezproxy.lib.ed.ac.uk/login?url=http://s.
Buckley-Marudas, Mary Francis, and Charles Ellenbogen. 2019. "Using YA Literature to Support Students as They Wrestle with Violence, Police Brutality, and Trauma: Engaging The Hate U Give." *The ALAN Review* 46 (3): 71–83.
Callner, Marty. 1999. *Jerry Seinfeld Live on Broadway: I'm Telling You for the Last Time*. HBO home video.
Cammarota, Julio. 2011. "From Hopelessness to Hope: Social Justice Pedagogy in Urban Education and Youth Development." *Urban Education* 46 (4): 828–44.
Chin, Elizabeth. 2007. "Power-Puff Ethnography/Guerrilla Research: Children as Native Anthropologists." In *Representing Youth: Methodological Issues in Critical Youth Studies*, edited by Amy Best, 269–83. New York and London: New York University Press.

Connors, Sean P. 2017. "An Invitation to Look Deeper into the World: Using Young Adult Fiction to Encourage Youth Civic Engagement." *The ALAN Review* 45 (1): 12–21.
Daniels, Harvey. 2006. "What's the Next Big Thing with Literature Circles?" *Voices from the Middle* 13 (4): 10–15.
Dejaynes, Tiffany, and Christopher Curmi. 2015. "Youth as Cosmopolitan Intellectuals." *English Journal* 104 (3): 75–80.
Delpit, Lisa. 2006. "Lessons from Teachers." *Journal of Teacher Education* 57 (3): 220–31. https://doi.org/10.1177/0022487105285966.
Draper, Sharon M. 2012. *Out of My Mind*. New York: Antheum.
Fitzgerald, F. Scott. 1925. *The Great Gatsby*. New York: Scribner's.
Gee, James Paul. 2001. "Identity as an Analytic Lens for Research in Education." *Review of Research in Education* 25: 99–125. http://www.jstor.org/stable/1167322.
Goodwinp, Bryan. 2010. "Research Says . . . / Choice Is a Matter of Degree." *Educational Leadership* 68 (1): 80–81.
Graham, Steve, and Dolores Perin. 2007. "Effective Strategies to Improve Writing of Adolescents in Middle and High Schools-A Report to Carnegie Corporation of New York." Washington, DC.
Griffith, Jason. 2017. *From Me to We*. New York: Routledge.
Gutting, Gary, and Elizabeth Anderson. 2015. "What's Wrong with Inequality?" *The New York Times*, April 23, 2015.
Hays, Alice. 2018. "What He Knows and What He Will Say: Voicing for Justice in All American Boys." In *Contending with Gun Violence in the English Language Classroom*, edited by S. Shaffer, G. Rumohr-Voskuil, and S. Bickmore, 81–87. Routledge.
Hurst, Heather. 2015. "Dodging the 'r' Word: Research as a Tacit Process." *English Journal* 105 (2): 96–101.
"Identity." 2020. Merriam-Webster.Com. 2020. https://www.merriam-webster.com/help/citing-the-dictionary.
Ivey, Gay, and Peter H. Johnston. 2018. "Engaging Disturbing Books." *Journal of Adolescent and Adult Literacy* 62 (2): 143–50. https://doi.org/https://doi.org/10.1002/jaal.883.
Ivey, Gay, and Karen Broaddus. 2001. "'Just Plain Reading' : A Survey of What Makes Students Want to Read in Middle School Classrooms." *Reading Research Quarterly* 36 (4): 350–77.
Ivey, Gay, and Peter H. Johnston. 2013. "Engagement with Young Adult Literature: Outcomes and Processes." *Reading Research Quarterly* 48 (3): 255–75. https://doi.org/10.1002/rrq.46.
Jimenez, Francisco. 1997. *The Circuit*. University of New Mexico Press.
Keen, Suzanne. 2006. "A Theory of Narrative Empathy." *Narrative* 14 (3): 207–36.
Keene, Ellin Oliver. 2007. "The Essence of Understanding." In *Adolescent Literacy Turning Promise into Practice*, edited by K. Beers, R. Probst, and L. Rief, 27–38. Portsmouth: Heinemann.
Krosoczka, Jarrett J. 2018. *Hey, Kiddo*. New York: Graphix.

Lesesne, Terri. 2007. "Of Times, Teens, and Books." In *Adolescent Literacy Turning Promise into Practice*, edited by K. Beers, R. Probst, and L. Rief, 61–79. Portsmouth: Heinemann.

Malo-Juvera, Victor, and Crag Hill. 2020. "The Young Adult Canon: A Literary Solar System." In *Critical Explorations of Young Adult Literature: Identifying and Critiquing the Canon*, edited by V. Malo-Juvera and C. Hill. New York: Taylor & Francis.

McElvain, Cheryl Marie. 2010. "Transactional Literature Circles and the Reading Comprehension of English Learners in the Mainstream Classroom." *Journal of Research in Reading* 33 (2): 178–205. https://doi.org/10.1111/j.1467-9817.2009.01403.x.

Miller, Donalyn. 2012. "Creating a Classroom Where Readers Flourish." *The Reading Teacher*, 66 (2): 88–92. Retrieved January 18, 2021, from http://www.jstor.org/stable/23322715.

Miller, Laura. 2004. "Why Teachers Love Depressing Books." *New York Times*, August 23, 2004.

Moje, Elizabeth, C. Lewis, and Patricia Enciso. 2007. "Examining Opportunities to Learn Literacy: The Role of Critical Sociocultural Literacy Research." In *Reframing Sociocultural Research on Literacy: Identity, Agency, and Power*, edited by C. Lewis, P. Enciso, and E.B. Moje, 15–48. Mahwah, NJ: Erlbaum.

Moley, Pauline F., Patricia E. Bandré, and John E. George. 2011. "Moving beyond Readability: Considering Choice, Motivation and Learner Engagement." *Theory Into Practice* 50 (3): 247–53. https://doi.org/10.1080/00405841.2011.584036.

Nilsen, Alleen, James Blasingame, Kenneth Donelson, and Don Nilsen. 2013. *Literature for Today's Young Adults*. 9th ed. Boston: Pearson.

Pajares, Frank. 2003. "Self-Efficacy Beliefs, Motivation, and Achievement in Writing: A Review of the Literature." *Reading & Writing Quarterly* 19 (2): 139–58. https://doi.org/10.1080/10573560308222.

Patall, Erika A., Harris Cooper, and Jorgianne Civey Robinson. 2008. "The Effects of Choice on Intrinsic Motivation and Related Outcomes: A Meta-Analysis of Research Findings." *Psychological Bulletin* 134 (2): 270–300. https://doi.org/10.1037/0033-2909.134.2.270.

Petrone, Robert, and Sophia Tatiana Sarigianides. 2017. "Re-Positioning Youth in English Teacher Education." In *Innovations in English Language Arts Teacher Education Advances in Research on Teaching*, 27: 89–105. https://doi.org/10.1108/S1479-368720170000027005.

Probst, Robert. 2007. "Tom Sawyer, Teaching and Talking." In *Adolescent Literacy Turning Promise into Practice*, edited by K. Beers, R. Probst, and L. Rief, 43–60. Portsmouth: Heinemann.

Probst, Robert E. 2017. "Impossible Days and Simple Texts." *Voices From the Middle* 25 (1): 49–51.

Pytash, Kristine, Katherine Batchelor, William Kist, and Kristen Srsen. 2014. "Linked Text Sets in the English Classroom." *The ALAN Review* 42 (1): 52–62.

Raby, Rebecca. 2007. "Across a Great Gulf: Conducting Research with Adolescents." In *Representing Youth: Methodological Issues in Critical Youth Studies*, edited by Amy Best, 39–59. New York and London: New York University Press.

Rowell, Rainbow. 2015. *Eleanor & Park*. Van Goor.
Rubin, Herbert J., and Irene S. Rubin. 2012. *Qualitative Interviewing: The Art of Hearing Data*. 3rd ed. Los Angeles, London, New Delhi, Singapore, Washington DC: SAGE.
Sensoy, Ozlem, and Robin DiAngelo. 2017. *Is Everyone Really Equal*. Edited by James A. Banks. New York: Teachers College Press.
Thein, Amanda Haertling, Megan Guise, and DeAnn Long Sloan. 2012. "Exploring the Significance of Social Class Identity Performance in the English Classroom: A Case Study Analysis of a Literature Circle Discussion." *English Education* 44 (April): 215–53. http://search.ebscohost.com/login.aspx?direct=true&db=eft&AN=74264976&site=ehost-live.
Thein, Amanda Haertling, Megan Guise, and DeAnn Long Sloan. 2015. "Examining Emotional Rules in the English Classroom: A Critical Discourse Analysis of One Student's Literary Responses in Two Academic Contexts." *Research in the Teaching of English* 49 (3): 200–23.
Trites, Roberta Seelinger. 2000. *Disturbing the Universe: Power and Repression in Adolescent Literature*. Iowa: University of Iowa Press.
Waal, Frans B.M. de. 2014. "What Is an Animal Emotion." *Annals of the New York Academy of Sciences* 1224 (1): 191–206.
Wolf, Shelby A., Karen Coats, Patricia Enciso, and Christine Jenkins, eds. 2011. *Handbook of Research on Children's and Young Adult Literature*. New York and London: Routledge.
Wolk, Steven. 2009. "Reading for a Better World: Teaching for Social Responsibility with Young Adult Literature." *Journal of Adolescent & Adult Literacy* 52 (May): 664–73. https://doi.org/10.1598/JAAL.52.8.2.

YOUNG ADULT WORKS REFERENCED

Abdel-Fattah, Randa. 2007. *Does My Head Look Big in This?*. Orchard Books.
Anderson, M.T. 2002. *Feed*. Cambridge: Candlewick Press.
Applegate, Katherine. 2015. *Crenshaw*. Feiwel & Friends.
Blume, Judy. 1974. *Blubber*. Macmillan Children's Books.
Crutcher, Chris. 2004. *Chinese Handcuffs*. Greenwillow Books.
Diamant, Anita. 2014. *The Boston Girl*. Scribner.
Doctorow, Cory, and Jen Wang. 2014. *In Real Life*. First Second.
Draper, Sharon M. 2015. *Stella by Starlight*. Atheneum Books for Young Readers.
Farish, Terry. 2012. *The Good Braider*. Marshall Cavendish.
Grande, Reyna. 2012. *The Distance Between Us*. Atria Books.
Gratz, Alan. 2017. *Refugee*. Scholastic.
Hiaasen, Carl. 2005. *Flush*. Alfred A. Knopf Books for Young Readers.
Hiaasen, Carl. 2006. *Hoot*. Yearling Books.
Jiménez, Francisco. 1997. *The Circuit*. University of New Mexico Press.
Jiménez, Francisco. 2002. *Breaking Through*. HMH Books for Young Readers.
Konigsberg, Bill. 2013. *Openly Straight*. Arthur A. Levine Books.

Krosoczka, Jarrett J. 2018. *Hey, Kiddo*. Graphix.
Levithan, David. 2012. *Every Day*. Knopf Books for Young Readers.
McCormick, Patricia. 2002. *Cut*. Push.
McCormick, Patricia. 2006. *Sold*. Little, Brown Books for Young Readers.
Medina, Meg. 2013. *Yaqui Delgado Wants to Kick Your Ass*. Candlewick Press.
O'Neal, Carolyn. 2015. *Kingsley*. Carolyn O'Neal.
Reynolds, Jason. 2016. *Ghost*. Atheneum/Caitlyn Dlouhy Books.
Reynolds, Jason. 2019. *Long Way Down*. Atheneum/Caitlyn Dlouhy Books.
Reynolds, Jason, and Brendan Kiely. 2015. *All American Boys*. Simon & Schuster.
Rowell, Rainbow. 2013. *Eleanor & Park*. St. Martin's Press.
Saeed, Aisha. 2018. *Amal Unbound*. Nancy Paulsen Books.
Shetterly, Margot Le. 2016. *Hidden Figures*. William Morrow Paperbacks.
Shusterman, Neal, and Jarrod Shusterman. 2018. *Dry*. Simon & Schuster Books for Young Readers.
Stone, Tamara Ireland. 2017. *Click'd*. Disney Book Group.
Vizzini, Ned. 2007. *It's Kind of a Funny Story*. Disney-Hyperion.

About the Author

Alice D. Hays has been an educator for more than twenty years, including eighteen years as a high school English teacher. Now a teacher educator, Dr. Hays combines her experience with adolescents with her knowledge of young adult literature to bring new ideas and approaches to educators in the field. As an assistant professor of education at California State University, Bakersfield, she works with the Kern High Teacher Residency program, where educators and preservice teachers show their desire to increase adolescent engagement while honoring student voices. This curriculum is born out of a desire to help teachers do just these things with and for adolescents.

Dr. Hays's work has been published in *The ALAN Review*, *Study & Scrutiny*, *SIGNAL*, and *The Journal of American Indian Education*. She has also contributed chapters to *Teaching the Taboo with Young Adult Literature* and *Contending with Gun Violence in the English Language Classroom*. She is an active member of the National Council for Teachers of English, and currently co-chairs NCTE's English Language Arts Teacher Educators Commission on the Study and Teaching of Adolescent Literature.